# The Very Best
# HEALING *Spices*

## Boost Your Health
## and Fight Diseases

# The Very Best
# HEALING *Spices*

## Boost Your Health
## and Fight Diseases

Céline Trégan

Céline Trégan

**The Very Best Healing Spices**

Cover photography and photography of recipes: Tango
Photographs on pages 10 and 12: Louise Bisson
Graphic design and layout: natalicommunication design
Layout of English version: Richard Morrissette
Translation: Patricia Boushel, Emily Raine

The publisher acknowledges the financial support of the Government of Canada through the Canada Book Fund (CBF) for its publishing activities and the support of the Government of Quebec through the tax credits for book publishing program (SODEC).

ISBN: 978-2-920943-80-3

Legal deposit – Bibliothèque Nationale du Québec, 2012
Library and Archives Canada, 2012

Les Éditions Cardinal
Montréal, Québec

Printed in Canada

# Table of Contents

*A Pharmacy at Our Fingertips* ............................. 7

*Herbs and Spices: Therapeutic Properties and Uses* ............................. 15

Garlic ............................................. 16
Dill ................................................ 18
Aniseed ........................................... 20
Star Anise ........................................ 22
Basil .............................................. 24
Cinnamon ......................................... 26
Cardamom ........................................ 28
Curry ............................................. 30
Caraway ........................................... 32
Celery Seeds ...................................... 34
Chervil ............................................ 36
Chives ............................................. 38
Cloves ............................................. 40
Coriander .......................................... 42
White Cumin ...................................... 44
Black Cumin ...................................... 46
Turmeric .......................................... 48
Curry Leaves ...................................... 52
Tarragon .......................................... 54
Fenugreek ......................................... 56
Juniper Berries .................................... 58
Ginger 60 ......................................... 60
Laurel or Bay Leaves ............................. 64
Peppermint ........................................ 66
Mustard ........................................... 68
Nutmeg and Mace ................................ 70
Oregano ........................................... 72
Parsley ............................................ 74
Chili Peppers ..................................... 76
Allspice ........................................... 78
Pepper ............................................. 80
Pink Pepper ....................................... 83
Licorice ........................................... 84
Rosemary .......................................... 86
Saffron ............................................ 88
Savory ............................................. 90
Sage ............................................... 92
Thyme ............................................. 96

*Herbs and Spices in the Kitchen* ............................. 100

**Spice Mixes**
Baharat ............................................ 101
Berbere ............................................ 101
Chat Masala ....................................... 102
Classic Curry ...................................... 102
Singapore Curry ................................... 103
Chinese Five-Spice ................................ 103
Antillean Colombo ................................ 104
Cajun Seasoning ................................... 104
Thai Red Curry Paste ............................. 105
Sambal Olek ....................................... 105

**Recipes**
Garlic ............................................. 106
Dill ................................................ 108
Aniseed ........................................... 110
Star Anise ........................................ 112
Basil .............................................. 114
Cinnamon ......................................... 116
Cardamom ........................................ 120
Curry ............................................. 122
Caraway ........................................... 124
Celery Seeds ...................................... 126
Chervil ............................................ 128
Chives ............................................. 130
Cloves ............................................. 132
Coriander .......................................... 134
White Cumin ...................................... 136
Black Cumin ...................................... 138
Turmeric .......................................... 140
Curry Leaves ...................................... 142
Tarragon .......................................... 148
Fenugreek ......................................... 150
Juniper Berries .................................... 152
Ginger ............................................. 154
Laurel or Bay Leaves ............................. 158
Peppermint ........................................ 160
Mustard ........................................... 162
Nutmeg ........................................... 164
Oregano ........................................... 166
Paprika ............................................ 168
Parsley ............................................ 170
Chili Peppers ..................................... 172
Allspice ........................................... 176
Pepper ............................................. 178
Licorice ........................................... 182
Rosemary .......................................... 184
Saffron ............................................ 186
Savory ............................................. 188
Sage ............................................... 190
Thyme ............................................. 194

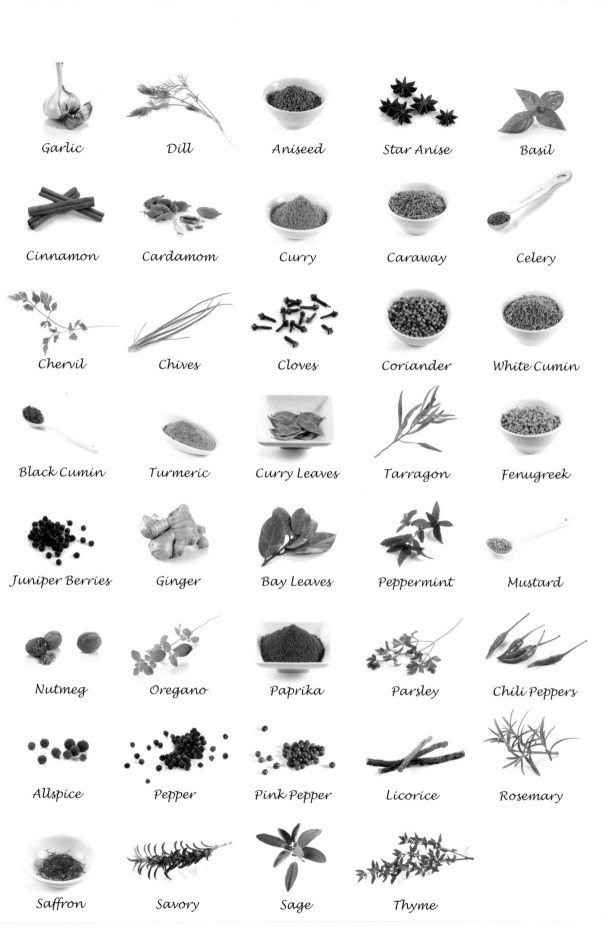

Garlic  Dill  Aniseed  Star Anise  Basil

Cinnamon  Cardamom  Curry  Caraway  Celery

Chervil  Chives  Cloves  Coriander  White Cumin

Black Cumin  Turmeric  Curry Leaves  Tarragon  Fenugreek

Juniper Berries  Ginger  Bay Leaves  Peppermint  Mustard

Nutmeg  Oregano  Paprika  Parsley  Chili Peppers

Allspice  Pepper  Pink Pepper  Licorice  Rosemary

Saffron  Savory  Sage  Thyme

# A Pharmacy at Our Fingertips

## The History of Aromatics and Medicine

When it comes to cooking, there's nothing more natural than using herbs and spices to season our food. We use them in our day-to-day cuisine and we take pleasure in the flavor boost they give to everything we eat. But how much do we really know about herbs and spices? What is their history and how do they get to our table? Herbs and spices have been valued as seasoning since the beginning of civilization, but they also played a vital role in daily life. We know that humans have been using aromatic plants for healing purposes since the Neolithic Period. In fact, spices were understood to have medicinal properties well before they were used to season food. Many ancient civilizations recognized the therapeutic qualities of herbs and spices and relied on them for their diuretic, purifying, stimulating, cleansing, and tonic properties, and used them to treat a wide variety of ailments.

The Assyrians and Babylonians of Mesopotamia added herbs and spices to food, medicine and perfume. They used herbs and spices as antiseptics and to mask the odor of infected wounds. The Egyptians treated heart problems with garlic and consumed juniper berries to improve digestion and get rid of intestinal parasites. The art of embalming required myriad spices and perfumes to slow the process of decomposition. In Greece, spices played a central role in funerary rites and medical procedures, and village physicians and healers added cumin to healing tonics and medicines. Hippocrates, the father of Western medicine, advocated the use of spices in cooking and famously declared: "let food be thy medicine, and let thy medicine be food." However, for two thousand years physicians and healers generally ignored this advice. Hippocrates encouraged eating herbs and spices to prevent plague, purify the liver, and improve the classical humors. Basil was used to treat epilepsy and fight against obsessive behavior, depression, and general malaise. Nigella was a common ingredient in the traditional medical practices of the followers of the Qu'ran and was even touted by the Prophet Mohammed as a cure for all ailments.

Spices were also the source of many unusual and generally ineffective folk remedies. During the 12th century, it was believed that keeping a nutmeg seed in a pocket would prevent broken bones as well as boils and skin irritations. A hundred years later, one French physician claimed that cinnamon stimulated the bladder and improved mood, strengthened the stomach, heart and brain, promoted good digestion, combated flatulence, and relieved stomach pain. Cardamom was also a common remedy for digestive problems, delicate stomachs, and nausea. Chinese and Indian apothecaries have been using healing spices since ancient times and often administer turmeric-based concoctions to treat dermatitis and improve liver function.

The Asian and European populations recognized the benefits of herbs and spices throughout history: they could be dried and easily preserved, were easy to transport, and possessed immensely valuable medicinal and antioxidant properties.

## A Passion for Spices

During the Middle Ages, the European population began exploring the indisputable enhancements spices brought to cooking. Europe had developed a strong

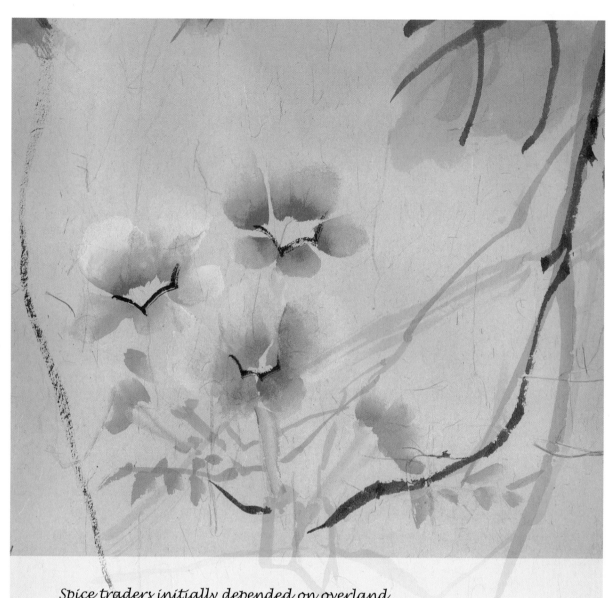

Spice traders initially depended on overland caravan routes, following the Silk Road from China across Asia to Europe.

passion for spices, and pepper, clove, cinnamon, nutmeg and mace, ginger, cardamom, saffron, sumac and galangal were in particularly high demand. They served as currency to settle debts and as ransom for kings, and were traded in exchange for goods. The wealthy desired spices for their sauces, dishes and soups, preferring white ginger, cloves, cinnamon, and above all, saffron.

*Le Viandier de Taillevent*, the earliest recipe collection known to exist, contains a repertoire of spices commonly used in the cuisine of the Middle Ages: ginger, cinnamon, cloves, grains of paradise (closely related to cardamom), long pepper, lavender, black pepper, cinnamon flower, nutmeg, bay leaf, galangal (similar to ginger), mace, cumin, sugar, almonds, garlic, onions, chives, and shallots.

Europeans were also fascinated by spices because of their symbolic representation. Spices come from the Orient, a faraway land associated with heaven on earth, and were thought to bestow both longevity and immortality. During the Crusades (1096-1270), pilgrims often returned to Europe bearing spices from the Holy Land. In the markets spice merchants sang the praises of their wares, cementing the reputation of spices as truly desirable commodities.

Although the history of spices is as old as civilization, it was only during the Middle Ages that the array and popularity of spices flourished, owing to their reputed therapeutic properties and extraordinary origins. These qualities seduced medieval Europe and the popularity of spices rose to new heights.

## The Spice Trade Route

In 16th century Europe, spices cost as much as jewels—they were truly worth their weight in gold, and played a pivotal role in the shaping of human history. Traders initially depended mainly on overland caravan routes and followed the Silk Road from China across Asia to Europe. Wealthy Arab and Venetian merchants controlled commercial activities, including the exchange of spices for silk, jewels, fur, wool, or precious ceramics. The price of spices increased during the long voyage, since conveying goods by camel or dromedary was extremely dangerous and cargos were often pillaged by unscrupulous thieves. In the Middle Ages, a pound of saffron cost as much as a horse, while a pound of ginger could be traded for a sheep. A pound of cinnamon was worth one cow, and pepper was worth a fortune in gold.

Already influential cities like Samarkand (Uzbekistan), Babylon (Iraq), Palmyra (Syria), Petra (Jordan), and Baalbek (Lebanon) saw tremendous growth and developed into major trading outposts. Because of the spice trade, Mediterranean cities such as Constantinople, Genoa, Florence, and Venice also became formidable powers. Arab merchants were the first to export spices from China and the Indies to the West and, allied with Venice, created a powerful navy and emerged as a driving force in the Mediterranean economy. Until the 15th century, the Middle East dominated the spice trade and profited enormously. The Portuguese finally broke the monopoly and took control of the sea route to India. They established outposts in the southern part of the West Indies and in Ceylon, where they harvested cinnamon as well as cloves and nutmeg, which only grew in the Moluccas, an archipelago discovered by the Portuguese explorer Magellan.

In 1492, Christopher Columbus convinced the Spanish monarchs to allow him to explore the West, a journey that resulted in the discovery of America. Six years later, Vasco da Gama commanded his pioneering voyage to Africa's Cape of Good Hope, arrived at Southwestern India's Malabar Coast, and, in 1502, sailed to Ceylon (modern-day Sri Lanka). In 1654, the French

During the Crusades, pilgrims often returned to Europe bearing spices from the Holy Land. In the markets, spice merchants sang the praises of their wares, cementing the reputation of spices as truly desirable commodities.

landed in India and created the French East India Company. A few years later, they introduced Oriental spices to their colonies in the West Indies (Guadeloupe and Martinique) and the Indian Ocean (Madagascar, Reunion, and Mauritius). In the 17th century, Dutch and British merchants established companies and trading posts on the coasts of Asia and, by the end of the 18th century, dominated the spice market.

### A Return to Herbs and Spices
It was during this period that Europeans discovered new ways of using herbs and spices. Cloves, nutmeg and pepper were still commonly used in cooking, but herbs and aromatic plants replaced other spices like mace, grains of paradise, long pepper, cardamom and saffron. French cooks used tarragon, parsley, chervil, basil, thyme, bay leaves, and chives to season dishes, added truffles and mushrooms to stuffings, sauces, and stews, and preferred capers and anchovies as seasoning for all kinds of savory meals. Rich sauces took the place of the lighter, acidic sauces favored during the Middle Ages, while sweet flavors, as well as cinnamon and ginger, were saved for desserts and pastries.

Cooks also started to recognize the importance of creating different flavors in dishes. This era saw the birth of a nouvelle cuisine, or new cuisine, that branched away from the popular sweet-and-sour cooking of the Middle Ages by separating sweet from salty.

Although the spice trade was a highly lucrative market, with the discovery in the 19th century of chemical substitutes and less expensive synthetic flavorings, the use of spices gradually declined.

### The Modern Age
By the end of the 20th century, most households had easy access to the different cuisines, flavors, and seasonings from across the globe. The way we eat had been forever transformed. The culinary arts and the food industry were becoming more liberal and chefs were given free range to create innovative dishes featuring spices as the keystone of their ingenuity.

As we know, plants held a very important place in medieval European medicine and diet. Nowadays, herbs and spices are the foundation of new and reputable healing techniques such as aromatherapy and phytotherapy, while the medical establishment is increasingly turning to herbs and spices in the formulation of new drugs. Modern chemistry is validating traditional knowledge.

Plants found in the forests of Asia, Africa, and the Amazon are currently the subjects of clinical trials that aim to isolate new compounds and potential applications for them. Pharmaceutical laboratories are also researching traditional remedies, many of which include the active ingredients found in herbs and spices. There is solid evidence that ginger, turmeric, green cardamom, pepper, saffron and cumin have antioxidant and anti-inflammatory properties that help the body fight diseases such as cancer. Including spices in a properly balanced diet will increase the body's ability to protect itself against these diseases.

### Fighting Illness with Herbs and Spices
Herbs and spices contain active ingredients that help slow the spread of cancerous cells. These cells multiply aggressively and are enabled by apoptosis, the genetically programmed death of damaged cells that is part of normal growth and development. The most effective way to fight cancer is to not only eat more fruits and vegetables, but also increase our intake of herbs and spices, which contain certain compounds not found in other foods. New research shows that herbs and spices may also help prevent arthritis, diabetes, cardiovascular disease, and Alzheimer's.

Certain herbs and spices contain compounds that protect cells from damage caused by free radicals, which are atoms linked to a series of disorders including cancer and cardiovascular disease and are thought by many to actually cause the aging process.

Herbs possess therapeutic properties that can treat major and minor ailments including problems of the liver and gall bladder, poor circulation, nausea and vomiting, and a wide range of digestive problems. Many herbs contain antioxidant phytochemicals that block free radicals, repair DNA damage caused by toxic compounds and stimulate the immune system by augmenting cellular apoptosis. Phytochemicals increase and maintain cellular interaction and, because of their high concentration of phenols, polyphenols, terpenes, flavones, or sulfurs, protect the body against illness and disease.

In the 11th century, the Benedictine abbess and respected herbalist Hildegard of Bingen compiled a list of remedies and recommended plant- and spice-based cures for health conditions that we still face today including cardiac and gastrointestinal problems, insomnia, and hair loss. Much like the North American aboriginals who passed down their knowledge of healing from generation to generation, Europeans recognized the therapeutic benefits of herbs and spices for treating minor ailments like toothache, colds, and joint pain but were unaware of the recently discovered potential of herbs and spices to affect more serious and even deadly diseases.

Recent studies have shown that fresh herbs act as antioxidants thanks to their high concentration of flavonoids. Some herbs, like basil, are rich in magnesium, and others, like cilantro, help fight breast and liver cancers. Reducing salt intake is

*Including spices in a properly balanced diet will increase the body's ability to protect itself against diseases.*

as easy as seasoning dishes with spices, herbs, lemon, and garlic instead of salt. Herbs and spices possess anti-inflammatory properties, have antifungal, antiviral and antibacterial activity, improve digestion and sleep, regulate the menstrual cycle, reduce gas and bloating, can be used as diuretics and purgatives, and can help combat cancer and cardiovascular disease.

## Revealing the Secrets of Mother Nature

This book reveals a modern approach to herbs and spices. In the first half of the book you will find a practical guide to 38 healing herbs that have been extensively researched and carefully tested to present to you the best way to take advantage of their curative and preventive properties. Each entry features a wealth of extraordinary health benefits, proving that these plants have astonishing natural medicinal powers and should be integrated into our daily meals.

The second half of the book includes a variety of culinary uses for these herbs and delicious kitchen-tested recipes that bring out their wonderful health-giving benefits.

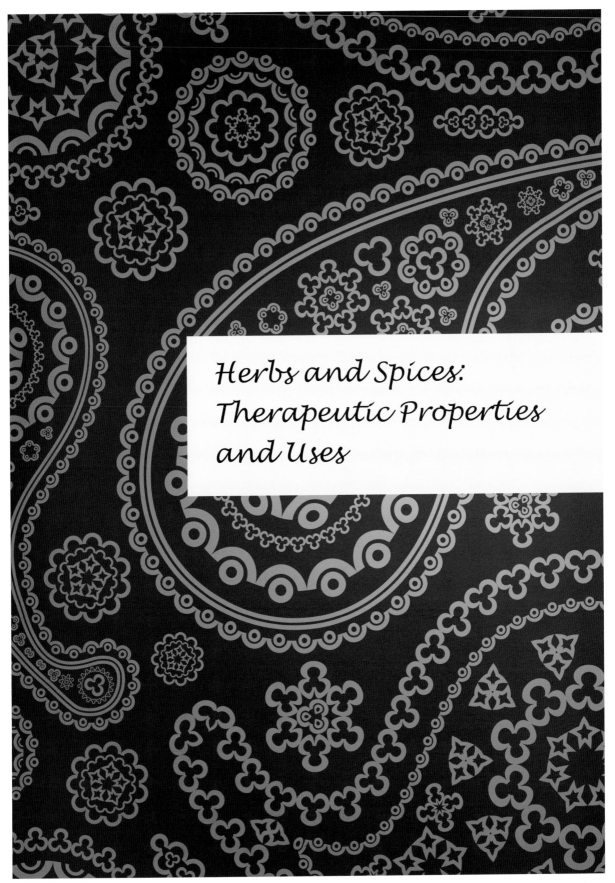

# Herbs and Spices: Therapeutic Properties and Uses

# Garlic

Garlic is not generally considered a spice, but because it is a classic cooking ingredient and one of the most therapeutic of all foods, it has definitely earned the crowning place at the top of our list.

Garlic is native to central Asia and is now primarily cultivated in China, South Korea, India, Spain, and the United States. It can be grown in most climates and types of soil. The bulb, or head, is divided into sections called cloves, which have pungent, spicy flesh. There are over thirty different types of garlic, most notably white, pink, and purple garlic. Spanish garlic has a similar, slightly mellower flavor.

## Therapeutic Properties

### Blood Pressure
Various studies have proven that garlic lowers blood pressure and increases triglyceride production and therefore reduces the likelihood of developing heart disease. It is also used to help treat asthenia, cardiac fatigue, tachycardia, arterial hypertension and other problems of the circulatory system.

### Allergies
Garlic is a powerful natural antihistamine. Garlic extract reduces the cellular response to allergens by 90%, making it four times more effective than leeks and eight times more effective than onions.

### Antibacterial
Garlic kills some strains of bacteria and is used for treating infectious diseases (influenza, typhoid, diphtheria), diarrhea and dysentery, pulmonary infections (tuberculosis, chronic bronchitis), asthma and emphysema, and whooping cough.

### Cardiovascular conditions
Garlic inhibits the formation of plaque on the arterial walls that cause atherosclerotic lesions. It has been found to reduce the level of cholesterol and free radicals in the body and prevent the hardening of the arteries.

### Diabetes
Garlic lowers basal insulin levels, regulates blood sugar levels, and lowers the body's resistance to insulin. It also helps the body convert glucose to glycogen to be stored in muscle cells. As an antioxidant, it protects the liver from damage that could increase blood sugar levels.

### Cancer

Garlic is rich in highly active antioxidants including organosulfur compounds and flavonoids that can capture free radicals, the instable oxygen molecules that damage cellular DNA. Like onions, garlic bulbs also contain certain sulfur compounds that can block the development of precancerous cells.

When garlic cloves are chopped or crushed, they release the compound allicin. Allicin produces sulfides, diallyl disulfide, and ajoene, which also prevent the spread of cancerous cells. Regularly consuming garlic or garlic extract strengthens the immune system and reduces the risk of developing many forms of cancer.

In a study published in *The American Journal of Clinical Nutrition*, researchers confirmed that eating raw and cooked garlic reduces the risk of stomach cancer by half and the risk of colorectal cancer by two-thirds. Another study revealed a significantly lower incidence of stomach cancer in inhabitants of China's Gangshang Province who consumed a ¾-ounce portion or more of garlic daily. The cancer rate in Gangshang province was found to be 13 times lower than that of other provinces where less than 0.03 ounces per day was consumed.

Garlic and onions also protect against mouth, throat, kidney and ovarian cancers, especially when combined with vegetables, particularly tomatoes. By eating more garlic, we lower our risk of developing larynx, prostate, and breast cancers.

## Therapeutic Uses

Experts recommend eating two cloves of garlic every day. Choose raw garlic over cooked garlic, as cooking it may destroy some of the garlic's beneficial properties. To preserve garlic's health-giving benefits, crush cloves with a mortar and pestle or with a knife blade. Add it to salads along with a dash of lemon juice instead of vinegar to release the ajoene, an effective anticoagulant found in garlic.

## Delicious Recipes

Reap garlic's healthy rewards by treating yourself to a tasty dish made with raw garlic and a sumptuous meal that uses 40 whole cloves!

**Forty Clove Roast Chicken**

See page 107

# Dill

Dill is an aromatic perennial plant native to the Mediterranean Basin and Western Asia. Dill is related to fennel and is often confused with the vegetable, as their leaves are similar in appearance. The name comes from the Old English *dile*, which may have originated from the Norse or Anglo-Saxon word *dyle*. It is a member of the *Apiaceae* family, which includes parsley, carrots, and cumin, and is a common ingredient in Scandinavian, Russian, central European, and North African cuisine.

Unlike fennel, the dill root usually only sprouts a single stalk. The plant usually grows to about 25 inches and has flat, ribbed, oval-shaped seeds. Dill seeds have a strong, slightly bitter flavor that resembles that of aniseed and a spicy, pungent aroma reminiscent of fennel, caraway and mint. The seeds contain carvone and anethole, two compounds that give the extracted essential oil its distinctive aroma.

## Therapeutic Properties

Dill is an extremely effective antioxidant. The anethol oil extracted from dill contains choline, an essential nutrient that helps maintain liver health by protecting hepatic cells.

Dill has long been used as a digestive aid; it eases the symptoms of dyspepsia (indigestion), gas, and intestinal cramps. Chewing on a few dill seeds alleviates abdominal pain by relaxing the smooth muscles of the intestines and helps relieve nausea.

### Caution
Dill essential oil should be taken in low doses and is not recommended for pregnant and nursing women.

## Therapeutic Uses

### In History
In the Middle Ages, dill was used as a charm against witchcraft.

### Today
Dill essential oil is used medicinally for its digestive, antispasmodic and sedative properties.

## Dill Digestive Tea

**Serves 1**

1 tbsp dill seeds

1 cup (250 ml) boiling water

• Add dill seeds to boiling water and infuse for 10 minutes.

Dill is a powerful diuretic when taken in large doses; limit intake to 3 cups a day.

*Delicious Recipes*

Salmon Gravlax with Dill

**See page 108**

# Anise

Anise, also called aniseed, is an annual plant that most likely originated in Asia and spread southwest to the eastern Mediterranean region. Its small white flowers grow in dense umbels and the pungent, delicately sweet oblong seeds from which anethole essential oil is derived are encased inside the dry fruit, or achene. Anise is often confused with fennel, dill, caraway, and star anise, but can be distinguished by its sweet licorice flavor.

## Therapeutic Properties

Anise contains polysaccharides and flavonoids and is rich in anethole essential oil, a common digestive aid. Its fruit also contains creosol and alpha-pinene, organic compounds that act as an expectorant. Aniseed can be used to treat coughs, indigestion, nervous stomach, respiratory spasms, nervous tension and insomnia, bronchitis, hiccups, and vomiting. It stimulates bodily functions, activates secretions, strengthens the heart, boosts the immune system, and increases nerve cell activity. Women use anise to treat menstrual discomfort and to increase milk production after giving birth.

### In History
Anise is one of the main ingredients in theriac, a medical concoction used as a universal remedy throughout the ancient world.

### Today
Anethol is a common ingredient in natural toothpastes and paregoric, or camphorated tincture of opium, a medication used for its antiseptic and antidiarrheal properties.

# Therapeutic Uses

## Anti-Stress Anise Infusion

**Makes 2 cups**

½ tsp aniseed

2 cups (500 ml) water

- Bring water to a boil. Add aniseed and continue boiling for 1 minute.
- Infuse for 10 minutes and strain.

Drink after meals. Aniseed is naturally sweet so no sugar needs to be added.

## Cough Control Tea

**Makes 4 cups**

1 tbsp aniseed

4 cups (¼ gallon) boiling water

**Preparation**

- Grind aniseed with a mortar and pestle, add to boiling water, and infuse for 10 minutes.
- Strain and drink between meals.

*Delicious Recipes*

**Aniseed Nut Cake**

See page 110

# Star anise

Star anise is a spice obtained from the *Illicum verum*, a small evergreen tree native to China and Vietnam. The tree's fruit is harvested just before ripening and dried in the sun. Each of the star-shaped fruit's eight points contains a glossy brown seed. Star anise seeds have a sweet, delicately peppery taste with hints of licorice and anise, but it is the tough, rust-colored husk that provides the spice's warm aroma. Star anise contains anethole, the same compound that gives anise its distinctive flavor.

## Therapeutic Properties

Star anise is a warm and moving spice. The pericarp of the plant's fruit (not the seeds) has a strong, pleasant perfume similar to that of anise and a mild, slightly sweet taste. It is widely used as a digestive aid, carminative, antispasmodic, and expectorant.

### In History

In China, star anise is known as eight horns. It was highly prized for its various properties.

### Today

- Star anise is used in the production of flavored liquors, most notably pastis.
- Star anise is a major component in the synthesis of the drug oseltamivir (Tamiflu), a major weapon against global influenza and avian flu.

## Therapeutic Uses

### Anti-Gas Infusion

**Makes 1 cup**

8 whole star anise

1 cup (250 ml) boiling water

- Pour boiling water over star anise and infuse for 15 minutes.
- Strain and drink after meals.

## Anti-Bronchitis Rice

**Serves 2**

1 cup (250 ml) white rice

2 cups (500 ml) water

3 whole star anise

- Bring rice and water to a boil.
- Add star anise to boiling rice, reduce heat, and cook over low heat, about 20 minutes.
- Discard star anise. Let sit for 5 minutes and serve.

*Delicious Recipes*

Mango Star Anise Cream

See page 112

# Basil

Basil, originally from Asia, is typically cultivated in warm climates but can also be grown indoors. Common sweet basil is an annual plant with pale to dark green leaves, although a purple variety also exists. Basil varies in flavor: sweet basil tastes lemony, while African blue basil has a strong note of camphor. Lettuce leaf basil, an ancient wide-leaf variety, is mildly sweet and highly aromatic, with notes of jasmine, licorice, and lemon. Basil cultivated close to the Indian Ocean contains estragole and small amounts of other terpenes (cineol, fenchol, linalool and methyl eugenol). Basil grown in Europe contains higher quantities of linalool and methyl eugenol, and African basil contains thymol.

## Therapeutic Properties

Like most plants in the *Lamiaceae* family, such as mint, thyme, marjoram, oregano and rosemary, basil contains essential oils rich in terpenes, which attract insects and defend the plant against harmful bacteria and mold. The silica and saponin found in basil have a beneficial effect on the urinary tract and reduce bloating. The plant's tannins and mineral salts aid digestion, promote healthy lactation, and are even an effective sedative! In addition, the eugenol component of basil oil is known to have anti-inflammatory properties, which helps alleviate chronic inflammation.

Basil helps relieve respiratory congestion due to its high concentration of camphor. A warm or cold basil infusion is excellent for soothing tired, itchy eyes caused by long drives or too many hours spent in front of the television or computer. The infusion can be used as an eyewash or applied with a compress, and should be made with fresh basil leaves. If the leaves are dried or ground, small particles can remain in the mixture and irritate the eyes, even after straining. (See recipe on the next page.)

### Cancer

Rosmarinic acid and ursolic acid are used by the body to prevent cancerous cells from spreading, and research suggests that basil leaf extracts destroy free radicals and inhibit the growth of cancerous tumors in animals.

### Diabetes

Basil lowers blood sugar, cholesterol, and cortisol levels, and regulates blood pressure by relieving stress. Various studies prove that basil is one of a group of medicinal herbs that show evidence of being able to help treat or prevent type 2 diabetes.

## Therapeutic Uses

## Basil Digestive Aid Tea

### Makes 1 cup

1 tbsp fresh basil leaves, chopped

1 cup (250 ml) boiling water

- Infuse basil leaves in boiling water and strain. Drink hot.

## Soothing Basil and Linden Eye Infusion

### Serves 1

1 tbsp fresh basil leaves

1 tbsp fresh linden leaves

1 cup (250 ml) boiling water

• Infuse leaves in boiling water and strain.

Use as an eyewash or apply to eyes with a compress.

## Infusion to Reduce Fever

### Serves 1

1 tbsp basil leaves

½ tbsp ground cinnamon

½ tbsp brown sugar

1 cardamom pod

2 cups (500 ml) boiling water

- Add spices and brown sugar to boiling water and infuse for 10 minutes. Strain.

Drink 1 glass every 2 hours.

*Delicious Recipes*

**Basil Pesto**

See page 114

# Cinnamon

South East Asia produces the majority of the world's cinnamon. The word cinnamon comes from the Latin word *canna* and first appeared in the 12th century, but the history of cinnamon goes back to remote antiquity. The spice is harvested by scraping off the outer bark of the cinnamon tree and removing the inner bark, which is then dried and cut for sale; the leaves of the cinnamon tree are used for essential oil. Ceylon and Chinese cinnamon are the most popular varieties: Ceylon cinnamon's light brown bark has a fine texture, a mildly sweet flavor, and dries into a single tightly spiraled roll, while thicker Chinese cinnamon bark is dark brown, slightly bitter, and curls up on both ends to form two small spirals. In the United States, Chinese cinnamon is the most commonly used variety, but it is generally considered to be of lower quality than Ceylon cinnamon.

## Therapeutic Properties

### Cancer and Heart Disease

In a recent study published in the *American Journal of Clinical Nutrition*, it was shown that ground cinnamon is ranked fourth out of the 50 foods highest in antioxidants per 3 ½-ounce portion. Cinnamon also contains the highest level of proanthocyanidins per 3 ½-ounce portion after cocoa beans, 20 times higher than cranberries. Proanthocyanidins function as an antioxidant by protecting blood cells and lipids from oxidative stress. Cinnamon is high in fiber and contains iron and magnesium, a mineral that helps protect the body from damage caused by free radicals often associated with heart disease and cancer.

### Arthritis

A recent study conducted by the University of Copenhagen found that out of two hundred patients who took a mixture of honey and ground cinnamon (1 tablespoon of each) every day before breakfast, seventy-three reported being completely pain-free after one week. After one month, almost every patient unable to walk due to arthritis had started to walk again without pain.

### Diabetes

The polyphenols found in cinnamon, when taken in small amounts, are known to improve the body's sensitivity to insulin, and the spice also helps lower blood sugar levels in people with diabetes. One Swedish study has shown that people who drink rice milk with cinnamon two hours after meals have a significantly lower blood sugar level than people who drink plain rice milk. In fact, as little as 1/2 tsp of cinnamon can lower blood sugar by 30%.

### High Cholesterol

Cinnamon lowers cholesterol and triglyceride levels due to the fact that these levels are partially controlled by insulin. In one study, scientists were looking at the effects of common foods on blood sugar and discovered, much to their surprise, that apple pie actually lowered blood sugar levels instead of raising them. They concluded that the regulating property was, in fact, cinnamon.

### Antiviral and Antiflu

Taken in tea form, cinnamon's antiviral benefits become significant in preventing the common cold and flu while also protecting against chills. Its invigorating properties are helpful to those who are convalescing or suffering from fatigue or loss of appetite, which is why it is recommended notably in cases of asthenia after a bout of flu.

Cinnamon's anesthetic, antibacterial and antifungal qualities are owed to the essential oil eugenol, which may act as a pain reliever when cinnamon is applied to some wounds in powder form. It also stimulates the uterus, the heart muscle and the respiratory system.

### Digestive Pain

Not only is cinnamon high in polyphenols and antioxidants, its fiber content accounts for over half its weight: 1 teaspoon of cinnamon contains ½ an ounce of fiber. Its bark bears fortifying properties that stimulate the salivary glands and gastric mucus, aid digestion and the evacuation of gases, appease stomach pain, and increase gastric juice secretion, all while stimulating the digestive system as a whole.

## Therapeutic Uses

## Antiflu Infusion

### Serves 1

1 cup (250 ml) hot water

1 tsp honey

1 tsp ground cinnamon

- Boil water and pour into a cup.
- Add honey and cinnamon.

### Advice for Diabetics

People who suffer from diabetes are advised to integrate cinnamon into their diet little by little, such as by sprinkling it on toast at breakfast.

*Delicious Recipes*

Chocolate Cinnamon Spice Cake

See page 118

# Cardamom

Like ginger and turmeric, cardamom belongs to the *Zingiberaceae* family. It is mainly cultivated near Southwestern India's Malabar Coast, although it is also grown in Cambodia, Vietnam, and Sri Lanka. Cardamom seed pods grow on the plant's aerial roots and are delicately handpicked, then dried in the sun. Each pod contains around fifteen aromatic seeds that smell slightly of camphor, with a touch of lemon and pepper. Indian sun-dried green cardamom pods are of the highest quality. The pods may become brown if oven-dried or white if treated with sulfur, as is the practice in the United States. Black cardamom or Nepal cardamom, also known as false cardamom, is larger and more plump than the green or true type, and has a more pronounced camphorated flavor.

## Therapeutic Properties

Cardamom has notable antiseptic properties and is markedly effective in treating respiratory infections, particularly asthma. It eases bouts of fever, headaches, cold symptoms and coughs.

### Cancer

Like pepper, cardamom is considered a highly valuable spice. The phytochemical compounds that are contained in cardamom essential oil have similar therapeutic capabilities to drugs. We now know that this spice is an anticancer food.

### Stomachache and Sore Throats

Cardamom has antacid and stimulating benefits. It has been popular in Scandinavia since the 10th century, when the Vikings brought it over to help cure sore throats, coughs, and heart pains. They would also use it to combat stomachaches, as would the Romans after their feasts. Cardamom is not only effective as a stimulant, but also as a natural remedy in cases of digestive troubles, particularly after a large meal, and of bloating.

### Halitosis

Cardamom is generally recommended to freshen breath and to combat the odors resulting from oniony and garlicky meals. It is used to prevent gum infections and certain throat ailments in North India.

# Therapeutic Uses

. . . . . . . . . . . . . . . . . . . . . . . . . . . .

### Gluten Intolerance

- Sprinkle ground cardamom on cereal or add to bread or cake recipes.

## Toast to Relieve Heartburn and Cramps

### Ingredients

1 slice raisin bread

1 tsp ground cardamom

1 tsp non-hydrogenated margarine

- Toast raisin bread, spread on margarine, then sprinkle with ground cardamom.

## Appetite-Enhancing Cardamom Tea

### Ingredients

2 cups (500 ml) boiling water

1 tsp fresh basil leaves

½ tsp ground cinnamon

½ tsp brown sugar

1 cardamom pod

- Boil herbs and spices and infuse for 10 minutes.
- Cool and drink from a small liqueur glass 2 hours before eating.

*Delicious Recipes*

**Indian Chicken with Pistachios**

See page 120

# Curry

Denoting both a mixture of spices and a variety of Indian dishes conceived during the time of the British East India Company, curry, from the Tamil term meaning sauce or cooked dish, is not to be confounded with curry leaves that are found on the *kariveppilai*, or curry tree (see page 52).

Varying by region, whether it comes from the Far East, India, or Mauritius, this savory combination of spices generally contains turmeric, ginger, black pepper, cumin, hot pepper, clove, cardamom, tamarind, fenugreek, and coriander. A wide variety of spices can also complement this mix. There is no definitive recipe for the standard Indian curry blend called *garam masala*, but rather hundreds that vary depending on region and on caste. Curries can be Indian, Chinese, or British.

## Therapeutic Properties

### Cancer

Researchers have observed that there are is a lower incidence of colon cancer in population groups who eat a lot of curry. It is likely that this could be attributed to turmeric, which not only destroys cancerous cells, but also prevents the creation of new ones. Further research leads to a link between turmeric and skin, blood, and breast cancers. On its own, turmeric is not easily absorbed by the system, yet research has shown that its absorption can be increased by over one thousand times thanks to the piperine found in a curry blend's pepper. Turmeric, which is responsible for curry's yellow hue, is an anti-inflammatory and could be used in the treatment of lymphoma, according to researchers in Kentucky and South Korea. Doctors have conducted experiments seeking various combinations of anticancer drugs to improve lymphoma patients' quality of life and to increase their survival rates. The abnormal growth of B-lymphocytes, cells that produce antibodies and proteins capable of fighting certain infections, can cause some forms of cancer in HIV/AIDS patients, notably Non-Hodgkin lymphoma, an aggressive form of cancer that, if found in the brain or once it has spread to several areas, is difficult to treat. Turmeric can lead to apoptosis in lymphoma cells when taken with absorption-aiding piperine.

## Alzheimer's

The risk of developing dementia is lower in people who eat two or three curry meals per week. According to a study presented at the Royal College of Psychiatrists' annual conference, curry could help prevent Alzheimer's and dementia thanks to its turmeric.
It appears that turmeric prevents the spread of plaque and amyloid proteins in the brain, both responsible for dementia.

*Delicious Recipes*

**Colombo Lamb**

See page 122

# Caraway

One of the world's most ancient spices, caraway was found in riparian cities dating back to 3000 BCE. Though it grows wild in every Canadian province, caraway is cultivated for its tiny aromatic fruit throughout Europe, Western Asia, India, the Middle East, and the United States. Sometimes referred to as meridian fennel and a member of the parsley family, its aromatic leaves are feathery and finely divided, and its swiveling root is thick and tapered. The plant has tiny white or pink flowers and yields crescent-shaped brown-reddish fruit. Just like cumin, its seeds are small, elongated and black. They have a bitter taste, close to that of anise and fennel, and are sold whole or ground.

## Therapeutic Properties

### Gas and Intestinal Issues
Caraway seed essential oil contains carvone, limonene and other terpenes, and is thus incorporated into several tonic drugs, and is also antimicrobial. Caraway is considered to be the most potent carminative in western phytotherapy (a carminative plant being one that prevents the formation of gas and facilitates its reabsorption). It promotes digestion and dispels intestinal parasites. Caraway stimulates the appetite and salivary, gastric and biliary secretions, encourages peristaltic movement with certain doses, and has notable antispasmodic properties.
The seeds can safely relieve infant colic. After a meal, a few seeds can be chewed or ground with a mortar then infused as a tea in order to release the essential oil. Caraway's antiamoebic and antiparasitic properties can help treat the flu if it is caught before reaching the intestines.

### In History
During the Middle Ages, caraway was a common ingredient in love potions and was often used to ward off infidelity.

### Today
Caraway is used by the food industry in the production of Munster cheese, made in the Vosges region in France. It is also used to make alcoholic beverages such as kummel, a popular Eastern European after-dinner drink.

# Therapeutic Uses

## Anti-Colic Infusion for Infants

2 tbsp caraway seeds

2 tbsp fennel seeds

2 tbsp chamomile flowers

2 tbsp peppermint leaves

- Infuse 1 tsp of the mix per 1 cup (250 ml) boiling water. Strain and let cool.
- Pour into baby bottle and allow baby to drink freely.

## Digestive Tea

1 cup (250 ml) boiling water

1 tsp ground caraway seeds

- Grind seeds and put in teapot. Infuse for 10 minutes.
- Strain and drink.

## Gas Relief Tea

1 tsp caraway seeds

1 cup (250 ml) boiling water

- In a small saucepan, pour boiling water over seeds, bring back to a boil and cook for
1 minute. Let cool for 5 minutes.
- Strain and drink after a meal.

*Delicious Recipes*

**Carrot and Caraway Spread**

**See page 124**

# Celery
## (seeds)

Originally from Europe's southern regions, it was only in the middle of the 19th century that celery became a common vegetable thanks to German cultivation. It was used in Russia and Scandinavia to flavor soups and sauces. Today, it is grown everywhere. Leaf celery is comprised of bulbous roots, green leaves and one stalk. The leaves sprout directly from the plump roots. Its fruit are tiny brown-grayish seeds that have a warm, slightly bitter flavor with a touch of nutmeg and parsley.

## Therapeutic Properties

Celery seeds are used to treat the flu, colds, insomnia, and digestive problems. They contain an active agent that lowers blood pressure by reducing stress hormone levels. Chewing or swallowing whole celery seeds stimulates digestion. Ayurvedic medicine classifies these seeds in its list of spicy and warming aromatic plants. They relieve nausea, increase bile production and are recommended to counter tobacco's disastrous effects on the system.

### Cancer
Both celery leaves and seeds contain several kinds of polyacetylenes, organic compounds once believed to be poisonous. Studies have since shown that some of these compounds have potentially beneficial properties. In vitro tests have shown that these polyacetylenes have the capacity to inhibit the proliferation of certain kinds of cancerous human cells. In animals, celery seeds have been shown to protect against the development of cancer cells, an effect attributed to the antioxidant apigenin. Celery is one of the principle dietary sources of the antioxidant lutein, in the carotenoid family. According to one study, people who increase their lutein intake are less likely to develop colon cancer before the age of 67.

### Joint Diseases
Celery is used in arthritis treatments because of its high organic sodium content, which inhibits arthritic deposits by maintaining lime and magnesium levels. Celery seeds taken in small doses can relieve gout, osteoarthritis, and urinary tract inflammation.

## Therapeutic Uses

### In History
Celery seeds were believed to help remedy dropsy and jaundice.

### Today
The seeds can relieve gout, rheumatic diseases, and urinary infections when taken in small quantities.

## Urinary Tract Infection Prevention Tea

1 rounded tsp ground celery seeds

1 cup (250 ml) boiling water

- In a small saucepan, pour water over celery seeds, bring to a boil, and infuse for 10 minutes.
- Strain.

Drink 3 times a day.

*Delicious Recipes*

**Baked Eggs with Celery Seeds**

See page 126

# Chervil

Chervil derives its name from the Greek *kairephullon: khairein* means to rejoice and *phullon* means leaf. Native to Turkey, Russia's southern regions, and the Caucasus, chervil is now grown everywhere. This aromatic plant belongs to the opiate family and is a close cousin to curly parsley. A common plant found in many gardens, its refined flavor recalls aniseed despite its rather volatile aroma. Chervil's stem is thin and delicate and by late summer, its neatly trimmed leaves turn pink-crimson. Its small white flowers form umbels that yield thin and elongated black fruit.

## Therapeutic Properties

When crinkled and rubbed onto insect bites, chervil leaves can dull pain and throttle allergies. When brewed, the flower heads can alleviate kidney congestion and breast engorgement during lactation. This aromatic herb is a purgative and diuretic agent, and is also effective against contusions when its crushed leaves are used with salt and vinegar as a poultice. Its stimulating properties having long been overlooked, the familiar and aromatic chervil is now known as a digestive aid and a cough suppressant.

### Antioxidant

Chervil is extremely rich in vitamin C, mineral salts, other vitamins, and the antioxidant carotene. We know that antioxidants attack free radicals, which cells produce in large amounts when in contact with pollution or UV rays. Antioxidants have protective properties that act against the harmful effects of pollution and UV rays, helping to slow the aging process.

## Therapeutic Uses

### In History

Chervil was known to stimulate the appetite and the ancient Greeks used it to flavor dishes. The Romans believed it to be a blood purifier, a digestive aid, and an overall strengthener, whereas in the Middle Ages, it was used to treat lazy stomachs.

### Today

Chervil is mainly known around the kitchen as a flavoring for salads, dips, sauces and soups. It is best to eat it raw in order to enjoy all its benefits.

Musky chervil, a variety with a taste akin to aniseed, is very effective against diabetes.

## Pre-meal Tea

1 tbsp dried chervil leaves

1 cup (250 ml) boiling water

- Cover leaves in boiling water and infuse for 10 minutes.
- Strain and drink lukewarm 1 hour before a meal.

## Cough Suppressant Tea

1 large handful fresh chervil

4 cups (¼ gallon) boiling water

- Cover leaves in boiling water and infuse for 10 minutes.

*Delicious Recipes*

**Asparagus with Chervil Cream**

**See page 128**

# Chives

Widespread across Europe and North America, chives are an aromatic herbaceous plant in the *Alliaceae* family that grows in large tufts and proliferates rapidly thanks to the pseudorhizomes in its roots. Their spiraling stems are long, hollow tubes that can grow up to one foot high. A chive's floral stem resembles a leaf topped by a dense inflorescence. The flowers vary in number and also in color, ranging from blueish to pink, and bear small spherical capsular seeds. Thymol (an aromatic monoterpene), carvacrol, and several other aromatic composites are the main ingredients in its essential oil.

## Therapeutic Properties

### Hypertension
Alliaceous plants are known for their diuretic properties, stimulating the kidneys to eliminate water and sodium thanks to their high potassium, water and inulin content. Garlic, onions, chives and leeks all possess such draining properties, contributing to long-term blood pressure regulation.

### Cancer
Chinese chives, more potent than the western variety, are known for their antibacterial and antifungal properties. Also used in India, Japan, and China, this variety's flat stems are used to flavor egg dishes, noodles, and soups. Alliaceous plants are linked to a reduction in stomach and esophageal cancers. One study also links the consumption of these plants to a lower risk of prostate cancer. Their role in the inhibition of bacterial growth in the stomach could decrease the development of carcinogenic compounds. Recent studies have shown that the allyl methyl sulfide in alliaceous plants can prevent cancers of the lung, liver, and colon, as well as the creation of blood clots. Chinese chives have been grown and consumed in China for over 3,000 years. Not only or they rich in carotenes and vitamins B,C and E, but in combination with its polysulfides, namely the allyl methyl sulfide to which onion and garlic owe its pungent odor, this herb acquires important antibacterial and anticancer properties.

## Therapeutic Uses

### In History

In France, chives were long used solely as an ingredient in a meat stew named civet, derived from *cive* (old French for chive). Chives were also once believed to cure rheumatism.

### Today

Chives are often recommended as a condiment to help lower blood pressure, as it has highly effective diuretic properties. In order to fully reap the benefits of the herb, adding salt to chive dishes is not recommended—not a tall order, as the taste of chives is potent and refined on its own.

## Headache and Cold Relief Infusion

2 tbsp chopped fresh chives

1 tsp ground ginger

1 cup (250 ml) boiling water

- In small saucepan, cover chives and ginger in boiling water and let simmer for 30 minutes.
- Strain.

*Delicious Recipes*

Shrimp and Chive Sauté

See page 130

# Cloves

The clove tree originated in Ternate, one of the Maluku Islands of eastern Indonesia. Today, it is industrially cultivated in Africa (Tanzania), Madagascar, and Indonesia. The cloves are this evergreen tree's floral buds, which are handpicked once they redden. They then turn brown as they are left to dry in the sun, becoming imbued with flavor and aroma and acquiring the rusty appearance of old nails. Cloves have an acrid, spicy, and persistent taste. Their odor is owed to an essential oil that evaporates once the cloves are ground but remains present in the floral peduncles and leaves, which are also harvested and dried on their own and either used whole or in powder form. Owing to their highly aromatic and acrid flavor, cloves must be used sparingly. They are most frequently used in oriental spice mixes, ground in Indian *garam masala*, in North African *ras el hanout*, or in Chinese five-spice powder. It is also one of the ingredients in kohl, once an ophthalmic ointment.

## Therapeutic Properties

The main elements of clove essential oil are eugenol, acetyl eugenol, some hydrocarbons, and traces of acetone derivatives and esters. Due to its analgesic and antiseptic properties, the eugenol extracted from clove essential oil is used in the medical and dental fields. It also plays a role in reducing both blood pressure and the myocardium's contractile strength without modifying the heart's rate or electric activity. Cloves prevent plaque buildup quite remarkably and are used as an anti-inflammatory agent, an effective antiseptic, a gastro-intestinal and uterine tonic, an antineuralgic, a local anesthetic, and a parasiticide. They can, however, be toxic in high doses. Cloves are used to cleanse the breath and to treat toothaches, and are known for their anesthetic, healing, and disinfecting properties. When eaten, they stimulate the appetite, aid digestion, and relieve gas.

### Diabetes
By increasing insulin sensitivity and improving the rate of glucose metabolism in people with type 2 diabetes, cloves play an important role in both the prevention and treatment of diabetes. Cloves' polyphenols, like cinnamon's, are responsible for these benefits.

### Premenstrual Syndrome
This syndrome, more widespread in the West than in the East, is linked to dietary consumption of isoflavones; consumption is only 1 to 5 mg in a daily western diet, compared with 35 to 200 mg in a daily eastern diet. A lab-produced clove extract could reduce breast pain during menstruation, one of the more widespread symptoms in western women.

### Antifungal

Carvacrol and eugenol are found in the essential oil extracted from cloves as well as oregano, and are renowned for their powerful antifungal properties that could be used to treat oral candidiasis. A study that evaluated clove oil's antimicrobial activity on a variety of pathogenic fungi, including those that cause urogenital infections, concluded that it was remarkably effective against opportunistic fungal pathogens such as *Candida Albicans, Cryptococcus neoformans,* and *Aspergillus fumigatus.*

## Toothache Relief Tea

- Drop 5 to 7 cloves in boiling water for 10 minutes, let cool, and use infusion as mouthwash before visiting the dentist.

## Analgesic Poultice

Relieves pain due to facial neuralgia, arthritis, rheumatism, bloating or gas, ulcers, sores, or colic.

2 tsp ground cloves

6 drops clove oil

6 drops water

White clay

- Mix ground cloves with enough clay for a poultice.
- Combine clove oil and water and pour onto clay.
- Add just enough additional water to make a thick paste. Wrap paste in gauze and apply to affected area.

### Caution

During pregnancy, clove oil can be toxic to an unborn child, despite its generally beneficial properties. It is not recommended for pregnant women.

*Delicious Recipes*

**Aromatic Apple Compote**

See
page 132

# Coriander

The word coriander is derived from the Greek *koris*, bug, and *andros*, man, due to the conception that the plant gives off the same odor as a male insect. In its plant form, coriander is also known as cilantro. First used in the Middle East, this umbellifer was then adopted into the kitchens of the Romans and Jews. Charlemagne later advocated the herb, as it shared a reputation with cumin and vinegar for preserving meats. It is also known as Chinese parsley for its resemblance to flat-leaf parsley. Coriander is a small plant, though its roots grow deep. Its leaves are fine and delicate, sinuated, flat, attached to a delicate feathery stem, and become more lobed higher up on the stem. The broader lower leaves emit a potent aniseed aroma. Coriander's white, pink, and lavender flowers are grouped in serrated clusters and yield light brown to beige globular fruit that smell of lemon and are used dried. Coriander essential oil is excellent for digestion, and was believed by the ancient Chinese to grant immortality.

It is impossible to trace the wild roots of coriander, but it is believed to have originated in Asia Minor or the Near East. Large-scale farms in the Ukraine, Russia, China, India, Pakistan, Morocco, Argentina, Mexico, and Romania cultivate it for its seeds. Its global yield goes mainly towards the preparation of curry powder, which contains 25% to 40% coriander. Its essential oil is also used for baked goods and meat products, in alcoholic beverages, in perfumes, and in pharmaceutical products in order to mask the bitterness of certain drugs.

## Therapeutic Properties

### Antioxidant

Due to its antioxidant properties and its beta-carotene content, coriander can help counter the effects of aging. It contains several antioxidant compounds, mainly phenolic acids, which are found in higher concentration in the leaves, as well as coumarins, terpenoids, and flavonoids, which are found in the seeds.

### Diabetes

Coriander helps control blood sugar levels in diabetics. In lab studies conducted on diabetic mice, research has shown that the addition of coriander seeds to their diet was effective in reducing blood sugar levels. The seeds stimulate insulin secretion and facilitate cellular absorption of glucose thanks to several chemical compounds. Clinical testing would be required in order to confirm the same benefits in humans.

### LDL Cholesterol

Coriander seeds could also contribute to the reduction of cholesterol levels. The levels of total cholesterol, LDL cholesterol—bad cholesterol—and triglycerides were reduced in lab rats when coriander seeds were added to their diet, whereas HDL cholesterol—good cholesterol—increased. Coriander could also lower the body's cholesterol through its role in decreasing the absorption of biliary acid in the stomach. Coriander's effects on human blood lipids would have to be clinically tested in order to conclusively confirm these preliminary results.

## Therapeutic Uses

Coriander seeds contain the plant's greatest medicinal properties. They give breath a sweet scent and also possess carminative properties, which means that they relieve gas, as well as diuretic and antispasmodic properties. The seeds stimulate gastric and hepatic functions, and provide effective relief of flatulence and bloating. Coriander alleviates abdominal pain and calms the nerves. The perfume and pharmacological industries use it to scent or improve the taste of some toothpastes and drugs.

The seeds have a stimulating effect when infused, aiding against aerophagy, digestion problems, and constipation. A coriander infusion can ward off diarrhea and other intestinal ailments, reduce toothaches, and be used as a mouthwash when cold. Coriander leaves exude a rather heady odor, restricting their use, and can cause dizziness if inhaled too closely.

## Digestive Infusion

- In a teapot, infuse 1 tsp coriander seeds in hot water for 5 minutes.

Drink before meals as a tonic, to facilitate digestion, and to stimulate the appetite.

## Rheumatic Relief Oil

2 tbsp coriander seeds, crushed

1 cup (250 ml) olive or hazelnut oil

- In double boiler, warm crushed coriander seeds in oil for 2 hours. Let cool and strain.
- Bottle and store in a dark place.

Use as a massage oil to relieve rheumatic and joint pain.

*Delicious Recipes*

**Carrot Coriander Soup**

**See page 134**

# White Cumin

Cumin plays an important role in spicy cuisine. There are two varieties: white cumin and black cumin, the latter being more rare. Hotter and spicier than caraway, cumin has a powerful aroma, and its seeds have a strong and bitter taste. Their acrid flavor can linger at length. The root of its name is found in the Latin *cuminum* and the Greek *kuminon*. A member of the parsley family of umbellifers, its leaves are dark green and tightly bunched and its flowers yield seeds that are harvested once yellow. These seeds are used whole or ground once dried. Cumin essential oil is extracted through distillation. White cumin's most important market is in Central Asia, though it is also harvested in Eastern Europe, Morocco (which produces the most fragrant and highly prized cumin), Iran, North Africa, China, and the Americas.

## Therapeutic Properties

White cumin stimulates the appetite, and is widely used to calm an upset stomach and relieve flatulence, colic, and diarrhea.

### Cancer
White cumin could help eradicate cancer cells as soon as they appear. As is the case with other aromatic herbs such as coriander, chervil, fennel, and vegetables such as carrots, parsnips, and mainly parsley and celery, white cumin has a high concentration of apigenin, a very powerful anticancer polyphenol. Apigenin's ability to inhibit the growth of a large number of cancer cells impacts the Western world's more common types of cancer, namely breast, colon, lung, and prostate cancers.

## Therapeutic Uses

### In History
In the Middle Ages, wearing a small bag filled with cumin seeds was believed to keep bad fortune and witches at bay. When consumed as an aperitif, it prevented bloating and digestive problems.

### Today
Cumin's reputation as an effective gas reliever still holds today.

## Digestive Aid and Gas Relief Infusion

1 to 2 tsp white cumin seeds, ground

1 cup (250 ml) water

- Boil water and pour over cumin seeds.
- Infuse for 10 minutes.
- Strain and serve.

Drink 2 to 3 cups a day as needed.

*Delicious Recipes*

**Creamy Hummus**

**See page 136**

# Black Cumin

Black cumin is native to Egypt and was used by the ancient Egyptians as a precious remedy. In fact, black cumin was even found buried in Tutankhamun's tomb. From the *Ranunculaceae* family of herbs, it is known the world over, and used mainly in China, India, and throughout the Arab world. It is also known as *Nigella sativa*, fennel flower, nutmeg flower, Roman coriander, blackseed and black caraway. It is renowned for its strongly flavored spicy and peppery seeds. They are thin, long, and brown, with a more delicate aroma than white cumin.

## Therapeutic Properties

Black cumin seed oil is used to treat various skin conditions. Known to the pharaohs, it has calming, regenerative, vitalizing, and anti-inflammatory properties. It was said that black cumin seed oil could cure all diseases except for death.

### Cancer

As a nutritional means of cancer treatment, black cumin is used to counteract the side effects of chemotherapy. Like ginger, it dulls nausea. It contains thymoquinone, which inhibits the spread of cancer cells. This same substance could also be helpful in slowing down tumor vascularization. A major study of the uses of black cumin oil in cancer prevention and treatment was conducted at the Cancer Immuno-Biology Laboratory of Hilton Head Island in South Carolina. It concluded that black cumin seed extract helps patients produce antibodies that contribute to increased interleukin production, a naturally-occurring protein of the immune system.

### Diabetes

Several studies have shown black cumin seed oil to have hypoglycemic properties. It reduces the blood's triglyceride and insulin levels by lowering the liver's glucose production, helping to regulate blood sugar levels in hyperglycemia patients.

## Heart Disease

Because of its antioxidant properties, black cumin seed oil is useful in both protecting against heart diseases and reducing the risk of cardiovascular diseases. It is known to have a hepatoprotective effect, to stimulate the immune system, and to lower blood pressure and heart rate. Through its effect on coagulation, it lowers cholesterol levels.

## Allergies and Skin Problems

Given its role in strengthening the immune system, black cumin increases the system's defenses against numerous pathogenic agents, namely bacteria, viruses, fungi and parasites. It would also be effective in fighting allergies and hay fever, as well as being useful in treating skin conditions such as eczema and psoriasis. The black cumin plant's numerous oils, including borneol, carvone, thymol and carvacrol, contain the following polyunsaturated fatty acids: stearic, linoleic, myristic, and gammalinolenic.

## Asthma

Black cumin, much like cortisone, has been proven to be an effective anti-inflammatory and bronchodilatory agent.

## Therapeutic Uses

### Gastrointestinal Aid Tea

**Ingredients for 1 cup**

1 tbsp black cumin seeds

1 tbsp honey

1 cup (250 ml) boiling water

- Pour seeds and honey in a cup. Pour boiling water over mixture, stirring until honey has melted.

- Cover and infuse for 10 minutes before straining.

*Delicious Recipes*

Black Cumin Quinoa Cakes

See page 138

# Turmeric

From the Latin *Curcuma longa*, turmeric's Arabic name is *khourkoum*, meaning saffron. When it is fresh, its spicy flavor is akin to ginger and actually quite different from saffron. Turmeric grows as the gnarled rhizome of a perennial herbaceous plant, and is yellow or lemon yellow depending on the variety. The most highly prized *curcuma longa* comes from Madras. It has a more bitter flavor than saffron that becomes more pronounced during cooking, and its color also becomes darker. It is an important ingredient in the Indian curry mix *garam masala*. Native to Indonesia and Malaysia, it is also grown in China, India, the Philippines, Taiwan, Haiti, Jamaica, and Peru.

## Therapeutic Properties

Turmeric is a very powerful and ancient antioxidant, which explains its widespread use in traditional medicine. It contains curcumin, which is known for its antitumoral, antioxidant, antiarthritic and antiamyloid effects, as well as for its anti-inflammatory properties.

### Cancer

Turmeric's curcuminoids are phenols that are responsible for its powerful antioxidant properties that safeguard DNA thanks to their role in diminishing the macrophage cells' nitric oxide production and in neutralizing existing free radicals. Curcumin has the greatest number of distinct anticancer effects of all studied vegetable molecules. It is used in preventative and curative treatments to abate existing cancers (particularly oral cancers, and those of the digestive tract, liver, breasts and skin). It suppresses the mutagenic effects of certain substances, namely those found in tobacco, and inhibits the development of nitrosamine, a carcinogenic substance. It also prevents the deterioration of certain tissues during chemotherapy treatments. Currently, one in six cases of cancer is directly linked to chronic inflammation. Through its role in reducing inflammation, curcumin succeeds in inhibiting cancer growth due to the fact that, contrary to most anti-inflammatory drugs, it is well tolerated by the system even in large doses and does not cause any side effects.

There is increasing evidence of the beneficial effects of this spice on certain cancers, particularly in cancers related to the digestive system. A study conducted at John Hopkins University in Baltimore concluded that turmeric intake, combined with quercitrin, a flavanoid found in apples, could reduce the growth of cancerous cells in colorectal cancers by 60%. Intestinal absorption of turmeric is problematic, but when combined with piperine, an active compound found in pepper, absorption increases by 154%. Cancer, Alzheimer's, and heart disease rates are lower in India than in Western countries due to the high daily intake of turmeric.

## Arthritis

Turmeric is the most powerful natural anti-inflammatory. A recent study conducted at the prestigious Sloan-Kettering Cancer Research Center in New York demonstrated that curcuminoids act by inhibiting an enzyme responsible for the inflammatory prostaglandins in the system. It thereby reduces inflammation by lowering levels of histamine and by increasing the level of naturally-occurring cortisone in the blood produced by the suprarenal glands. Turmeric acts by inhibiting the synthesis of inflammatory substances. In concordance with essential fatty acids, they mutually reinforce the other's anti-inflammatory activities. Unlike certain synthetic anti-inflammatory drugs, turmeric does not inhibit prostacyclin, an important factor in preventing vascular thromboses. Turmeric is a natural antibiotic as well as an excellent purifier and tonic. It regulates metabolism, cleans the system, thins the blood and purifies the liver by stimulating biliary functions.

Curcuminoids offer the double advantage of having effective anti-inflammatory properties as well as having no side effects, unlike most standard anti-inflammatory drugs such as aspirin. People who suffer from inflammatory diseases such as arthritis, which aspirin relieves, as well as those who have been accustomed to taking one aspirin a day to maintain their health, now have a viable natural option. Turmeric can treat rheumatoid arthritis as well as other inflammatory conditions such as asthma, multiple sclerosis, inflammatory bowel disease, and osteoporosis.

## Heart Disease

Turmeric helps treat thrombophlebitis thanks to its anti-inflammatory and blood thinning properties. It also contributes to lowering cholesterol levels in the blood and to increasing the blood's fluidity by disrupting plaque aggregation, a natural process by which blood cells bind themselves together. It prevents lipid peroxidation, particularly the peroxidation of cholesterol. When cholesterol oxidizes, it develops into artery-blocking atheromatous deposits. Smoking and diabetes accelerate the oxidization of cholesterol and harden the arteries, and resulting artheromas accumulate on artery walls. Certain spices, namely cinnamon, cloves, and turmeric could help diabetics to process carbohydrates and help smokers improve cardiovascular strength.

## Alzheimer's

Turmeric's antioxidant effects protect the brain and reduce neurodegenerative lesions by not only destroying the protein deposits that are responsible for the degeneration of certain brain cells in cases of Alzheimer's disease, but also by preventing them from forming. These effects could explain the low incidence of the disease in India, where curry, and therefore turmeric, is widely used as a culinary ingredient, colorant, and preserving agent.

# Turmeric

## Antibacterial, Antifungal, and Antiparasitic

Turmeric is an excellent analgesic and a powerful healing agent used for centuries for a wide variety of skin conditions, including external and internal sores, scars from operations, and cutaneous injuries. It is also equally as effective in preventing infection and relieving pain. Turmeric, much like cayenne pepper, blocks the body's pain messages. Recent studies have shown it to have an antiviral effect and to stimulate infection-fighting white blood cells. Turmeric prevents the growth of bacteria that cause amoebic dysentery, gangrene or necrotizing enteritis, staphylococcal and streptococcal infections, and bacillus, and of several pathogenic fungi. It can also be used to fight infections by inhibiting the production of certain bacterial toxins that are particularly dangerous to the system, such as aflatoxins produced by the fungus that grows on poorly preserved food.

## Therapeutic Uses

### In History

Turmeric has been used to treat skin conditions and inflammatory diseases for centuries.

### Today

Turmeric is a known as a formidable anticancer food, though it also combats the signs of aging and protects the immune system.

---

## Turmeric Smoothie

### Ingredients for 1 cup

½ cup (125 ml) light coconut milk or soymilk

½ cup (125 ml) fresh fruit
(strawberries, kiwis, citrus)

1 tsp turmeric

¼ tsp black pepper

### Preparation

For a smooth and refreshing cocktail, combine ingredients and consume immediately in order to take advantage of turmeric's health-giving benefits. For a nourishing vegetable drink, substitute your choice of vegetables for fruit, and water for milk. Try it with spinach, tomatoes, parsley, celery stalks, or cabbage leaves.

## Boil Relief Poultice

### Ingredients

1 onion

1 tsp turmeric

1 tsp ghee (clarified butter)

- Cook onion in a pan over medium heat until lightly golden. Puree with turmeric and ghee.

Apply poultice directly to the boil.

## Sprain, Strain, and Tendinitis Relief Paste

(reduces inflammation and swelling)

### Ingredients

½ cup (125 ml) or more turmeric

Water

Sea Salt (optional)

- Mix enough turmeric powder in water to obtain a thick paste. Apply as a compress.
- For considerable swelling, sea salt can be added (2 parts turmeric to 1 part salt).

**Warning! Turmeric will stain hands.**

## Dermatitis and Burn Relief

(relieves itching)

### Ingredients

1 tbsp turmeric

1 tbsp aloe vera gel

- Mix turmeric with aloe vera gel and apply directly to the lesion.

*Delicious Recipes*

**Lentil Soup**

See page 142

# Curry
## (leaves)

The curry tree, or *kariveppilai*, belongs to the *Rutaceae* family and grows 15 to 30 feet tall. Its leaves are known as curry leaves, not to be confused with the spice blend (see page 103). Its trunk and branches are quite slender and its leaves are dark green, rather small, and have a pungent, spicy odor. Once grilled and reduced to a powder, they are sometimes used in *garam masala* mixes, which acquire different names depending on the region. In North India, for example, it is called *masala*, which means mixture. Curry leaves are mainly composed of glucosides, alkaloids, essential oils, and tannins. The *kariveppilai*, native to tropical Asia, grows wild in Northern Thailand, and is harvested in Malasia as well as in all Southeast Asian countries, Southern India, Burma, Thailand, and Vietnam. It is unknown in the Caribbean Islands, though it has nearly become invasive in Reunion Island gardens.

## Therapeutic Properties

Curry leaves increase gastric secretions and relieve nausea, indigestion and vomiting. They are recommended against diarrhea and dysentery, and in India, are used to combat premature graying. Curry leaves are also used in poultices to treat burns and sores. The curry tree's roots, bark and leaves are used medicinally, both internally and externally. Infused, the leaves are known to lower blood pressure.

### Diabetes

Researchers at King's College in London have found that curry leaf extract could be helpful in controlling diabetes. Laboratory tests conducted on the curry leaf (used in India and in ayurvedic medicine) revealed a link between a reduction in blood sugar levels and an enzyme found in the leaves. This enzyme, alpha amylase, acts in the pancreas during digestion and transforms starch into sugar.

## Note

Strictly speaking, curry mixes and curry leaves do not present therapeutic uses. However, in the second part of the book, you will find recipes that were developed to fully enjoy their beneficial properties.

*Delicious Recipes*

**Pork and Potato Curry**

**See page 144**

# Tarragon

Known as dragon's wort or dragon herb, tarragon is a perennial aromatic herb in the *Asteraceae* family. Its stiff stem's long and thick leaves are very fragrant. Tarragon is rich in essential oils and is therefore very aromatic, exuding a strong and unique peppery aniseed-like perfume. Dioscorides and Avicenna claimed that the plant treated snake bites, and its name, *dranculus* (little dragon), originates from this belief as well as from the shape of its serpentine roots.

Tarragon is a mugwort, a genus that comprises three hundred species, namely absinthe, citronella, genepi, and common wormwood. The most common varieties are Russian tarragon, weaker in flavor and odor, and French tarragon, very fragrant and aromatic. Native to Central Asia, tarragon is one of the many herbs introduced to Europe by crusaders returning from the Near East. It spread across Europe in the 15th century thanks to monks who cultivated it in their medicinal gardens.

## Therapeutic Properties

Tarragon is used primarily to treat digestive troubles such as aerophagy, slow digestion, gastritis and colitis, hiccups, and travel sickness, as well as premenstrual and menstrual cramps. It also has antiviral and antiallergic properties and is used to relieve cramps, muscular spasms or spastic coughs, and asthma related to allergies. Researchers have found two types of benzodiazepines in tarragon, which are substances generally used to treat anxiety and insomnia. Studies have shown that tarragon cultivated in a sterile environment could synthesize these substances, which can bind themselves *in vitro* to specific receptors in the human brain. Tarragon's naturally produced benzodiazepines could have an equally important activity as their synthetic counterparts.

### Cancer
American scientists have examined the properties of artemisinin, a molecular compound found in the wormwood shrub, a plant in the same family as absinthe and tarragon that is used in Chinese medicine chiefly as an antimalarial. Artemisinin is active against multiresistant strains of plasmodium (the organism known as malaria) through interaction with the metallic ions that are present in high levels in this disease. Because cancerous cells also contain a high concentration of metallic ions, researchers have started trial testing artemisinin as an anticancer drug and have observed that cancer could be completely eradicated in an organism within eight hours in the case of leukemia, and within sixteen hours in the case of breast cancer. In addition, artemisinin has the advantage of not attacking normal cells.

## Therapeutic Uses

### In History

In the 13th century, tarragon was strictly used to cleanse the breath. Three centuries later, it was discovered to be a useful treatment for dog bites and an effective stimulant.

### Today

Studies are currently being conducted to better understand the therapeutic properties of the substances found in tarragon, namely coumarin, which is believed to have promising benefits in the treatment of allergies.

## Appetite Stimulating Wine

1 handful fresh tarragon

1 bottle good red wine

1 tsp maple syrup or honey

- In a carafe, combine tarragon and red wine. Leave to steep dry, dark place for about 15 days.
- Strain and sweeten lightly with maple syrup or honey.

Drink a small glass before a meal.

## Digestive Aid Tea

### Ingredients for 1 cup

1 tsp fresh tarragon leaves

1 cup (250 ml) boiling water

- Pour boiling water over tarragon leaves, cover, and infuse for 5 to 7 minutes.
- Strain and serve.

Encourages digestion and eases colic and constipation.

*Delicious Recipes*

**Green Vegetable and Tarragon Soup**

See page 148

# Fenugreek

Fenugreek belongs to the *Fabaceae* family, along with peas and clovers; the name literally means Greek hay because the Romans used it as livestock feed. This small herbaceous plant grows 8 to 20 inches tall, yields tough, angular, oblong yellow seeds that exude an aroma of freshly cut hay and have a bitter, sweet-and-sour flavor with a caramel aftertaste. The seeds' characteristic aroma is brought out by roasting.

Fenugreek grows wild in North Africa and is cultivated in India, Egypt, Lebanon, Argentina, and France. It is widely used as a spice in Turkey, the Arab-speaking world and in India. It is a staple in curry mixes and is a key ingredient in *garam masala*, along with ginger, cinnamon and cardamom.

## Therapeutic Properties

Fenugreek powder was traditionally used to treat sores, bronchitis, digestive problems, arthritis, liver problems and reproductive system issues in men. Its principal chemical components are saponins, which are linked to appetite stimulation, flavonoids, proteins and phosphorus, to which its neuromuscular stimulant properties are owed, magnesium, carbohydrates, and finally, saponin steroids, which contribute to the synthesis of cholesterol and sex hormones. It also boasts a mucilage content of up to 40%. Mucilage is a substance that becomes gelatinous when mixed with water and gives fenugreek its property of calming inflamed or irritated tissues. It helps slow muscle wasting in the elderly and stimulates the appetite.

### Cancer
In China, fenugreek is used to treat cervical cancer. It is also believed to help prevent the onset of certain cancers, namely of the colon, breast and gallbladder.

### Diabetes
Fenugreek is used to treat diabetes and malnutrition in India and the Middle East. It has a positive effect on blood sugar control and therefore protects the liver and kidneys from damage, regulates insulin production, and helps the system better use its blood sugars. Fenugreek increases insulin production while lowering triglyceride levels. At Jaipur's Center for Diabetes Research in India, it was found that fenugreek extract lowered blood sugar levels and decreased insulin resistance in patients with type 2 diabetes.

## Bad Cholesterol and Cardiovascular Disease

While raising HDL (good cholesterol) levels, fenugreek lowers overall cholesterol levels. It could play a role in preventing cardiovascular diseases, which pose a particular threat to diabetics.

## Arthritis

Belgian researchers conducted tests in India that confirmed fenugreek's mild anti-inflammatory properties, underlining its use against arthritis and other inflammatory ailments. Fenugreek sprouts are rich in vitamin E, iron and sulfur. They help in the treatment of arthritis and bronchitis symptoms, and can increase milk production in breastfeeding mothers. Used in a poultice to treat arthritis, a finely ground fenugreek seed reduction (used in similar ways as flax flour) can have a surprising effect against inflammations. This concoction is particularly effective against sinusitis, bronchitis and inflammatory arthritis.

# Therapeutic Uses

### In History

During the Middle Ages, fenugreek was believed to prevent hair loss.

### Today

Fenugreek's numerous disease-fighting properties are being actively studied, specifically its role in fighting cancer, diabetes, and cardiovascular diseases.

# Appetite Stimulating Brew

2 tsp fenugreek seeds

1 cup (250 ml) boiling water

- Add seeds to boiling water and simmer for 10 minutes.
- Strain.

Drink 2 to 3 cups a day to stimulate the appetite, for no longer than 1 week.

## Sprouted Seeds

Fenugreek seeds are tough, keep well, and can be eaten dried or sprouted. They will sprout overnight in water and can be eaten plain or in prepared dishes.

*Delicious Recipes*

Spiced Lamb

See page 150

# Juniper Berries

Juniper berries are the fruit of the coniferous juniper, a shrub-like plant whose evergreen needles are stiff and spiky, and of a grey-green to green-blue hue. The juniper's appearance varies according to its location. Some grow tall, like the cypress tree, reaching up to 15 feet in height, whereas others grow as bushes or low-spreading shrubs. Its round, fleshy, pea-sized berries ripen from green to deep purple over the course of 2 to 3 years. Ripe berries are coated in a waxy matte film, have a star-like fissure at their head, and contain three seeds in the shape of a trihedron. These seeds have a peppery, bitter, woody and mildly resinous flavor and are left to dry in the sun. Every part of this plant is highly aromatic.

Juniper berries are rich in sugar, resin, and a pleasantly fragrant essential oil that contains mucilage, tannins, some organic acids and many mineral salts. Hailing from the boreal regions of the Northern Hemisphere, the plant grows wild in arid, sandy, or rocky soil throughout North America, Asia and Europe. Crafty medieval spice traders sold it as black pepper: given the resemblance of the two spices, the more common and affordable juniper berries would be mixed in with the more precious pepper.

## Therapeutic Properties

Medicinal use of the common juniper berry goes far back to the time of the ancient Greeks, Romans and Arabs. Cato the Elder referred to juniper berries as the fundamental elements in a diuretic wine. Ancient Egyptians recognized the shrub's benefits and used it as a diuretic and sudorific. Emperor Nero's doctor, Dioscorides, considered juniper's diuretic properties as helpful to the stomach and the bronchial tubes. The main component of the juniper berry is an essential oil rich in terpenic hydrocarbons, namely pinene and terpineol, as well as a mix of bitters known as juniperin.

### Arthritis

The juniper cleanse is to autumn what the dandelion cleanse is to spring. Popular throughout Europe, this treatment promotes the elimination of uric acid and is highly effective in relieving arthritis, gout and all other rheumatic diseases. It appears that the combination of the dandelion and juniper cleanses in spring and fall increases mobility in affected limbs and areas while relaxing stiffness and inhibiting the growth of new lesions. This treatment is only effective if followed strictly, year after year.

### Diabetes

Recent studies have shown juniper berries to help prevent diabetes through their impact on blood sugar levels. The essential oil of a certain variety of juniper contains compounds that are known to have an effect on plaque deposits and to act as a vasorelaxant.

## Therapeutic Uses

### In History

In Egypt, juniper berries were used to combat intestinal parasites and as a digestive aid. They were used to purify the liver and the classical humors in Greece.

### Today

Juniper berries are attributed with great disease-fighting effects, useful in cases of liver and gallbladder diseases. They are also credited with fighting bacteria and used in treating lung ailments.

## Blood-Cleansing Infusion

### Ingredients

8 to 10 juniper berries

2 cups (500 ml) boiling water

- Pour boiling water over berries and infuse for 10 minutes.
- Strain and drink 3 glasses a day.

Do not exceed a 6-week cleanse period, given the risk of kidney irritation that occurs with excessive consumption of juniper berries.

*Delicious Recipes*

**Quail with Juniper Berries**

See page 152

# Ginger

Ginger owes its name to the Sanskrit *shringavera*, which means "shaped like a deer's antler." The linguistic development can be traced thereafter from the Greek *ziggiberis* to the Latin *zingiber* to the French *gingibre*, which became *gingembre*, and finally, to the English word ginger. It is a perennial tropical and herbaceous plant that grows from a rhizome up to 5 feet in height. The fleshy rhizomes vary in size and color, from a sandy golden to yellow, white, or red, depending on the plant's origin. The highly aromatic pulp is spicy, peppery, and can cause a burning sensation on the tongue.

The fresh rhizome, or green ginger, is the most commonly used part of the plant; it exudes a lemony and camphorated aroma that fades as it dries, leaving mostly its spice. It is covered in a layer of thin skin that is edible when the rhizome is young and fresh. Its essential oil is used to make certain perfumes. The most widely used variety is Jamaican ginger, known for its delicate aroma. The Australian variety has a much sweeter, more lemony flavor, whereas African ginger from Nigeria and Sierra Leone is more full-bodied and markedly camphorated. The latter variety is used in the production of essential oil and oleoresin. Indian ginger tastes quite lemony and is generally dried.

## Therapeutic Properties

Ginger contains no less than forty antioxidants, and many are heat-resistant and are actually released—not destroyed—during cooking. When ginger is heated, its antioxidant activity increases and is further amplified when combined with garlic and onion.

### Cancer

Two polyphenols in ginger are the compounds responsible for its cancer-preventing properties: gingerol and paradol. Paradol is noted for its antioxidant and antitumor activity. Gingerol, found mostly in fresh ginger, plays a more targeted role in protecting against cancers caused by UVB rays and in slowing down the spread of colorectal cancer. In a Michigan University study, ginger solutions were introduced to cultures of ovarian cancer cells, and it was concluded that with the ginger treatment, cancer cells were destroyed more effectively through the processes of autophagy and apoptosis than they were with chemotherapy treatments. The problem of chemotherapy resistance can be avoided through the use of ginger, which can also be helpful in the treatment of ovarian cancer.

## Rheumatic Diseases

Ginger, turmeric, and galanga, all belonging to the *Zingiberaceae* family, are the most active antioxidant and anti-inflammatory spices. Ginger has long been used to treat arthritis and bursitis. In cases of severe rheumatic illness, ginger, thanks to curcumin's active properties, has been shown to be as effective in treating postoperative pain as standard anti-inflammatory drugs. Ginger, however, possesses an additional benefit—unlike drugs, it protects the digestive tract.

A team of researchers at the University of Miami has proven ginger's effectiveness in relieving knee pain in patients suffering from degenerative arthritis. The medical journal Arthritis and Rheumatism published a noteworthy clinical study in which patients suffering from degenerative arthritis in the knee were given fresh ginger for 6 weeks. At the end of the study, researchers observed that those who took the ginger moved with greater ease, that their pain was less intense, and their articulations were less stiff.

## Bad Cholesterol

A regular intake of ginger lowers cholesterol, triglyceride, fatty acid, and phospholipid levels, and prevents the accumulation of blood platelets while activating the immune system.

## Alzheimer's

Gingenol, an oleoresin found in ginger, is responsible for its spicy flavor. It possesses anti-inflammatory and antioxidant properties, and converts to shogaol when ginger is dehydrated. It is this phenol that protects cells as Alzheimer's progresses. Dried or ground ginger contains more of this compound than fresh ginger.

## Colds, Flu, and Asthma

A natural antihistamine, ginger is known for is decongestant properties and its ability to ward off respiratory infections if taken as soon as the first symptoms of a cold or flu appear. Several studies have shown that the gingenol and shogaol it contains have cough suppressant, analgesic and antipyretic properties. If taken at the onslaught of a migraine, ginger can block the prostaglandins that cause the arteries in the brain to constrict.

*Delicious Recipes*

**Ginger Orange Salmon**

See page 154

# Ginger

### Nausea

Ginger's gingenol and shogaol help reduce agitation in the stomach. Gingenol, a chemical compound whose properties resemble those of the capsaicin found in chili peppers, prevents spasms in the digestive system's smooth muscle tissues while encouraging bile secretion. Ginger rhizome is effective in treating digestive problems and prevents nausea caused by travel sickness. An intake of between 0.017 ounces and 0.05 ounces of ground ginger in capsule form can effectively treat nausea and vomiting during pregnancy. A dose of 0.035 ounces of ground ginger (or 0.35 ounces of fresh ginger) could help prevent postoperative nausea and vomiting.

## Therapeutic Uses

### In History

Chinese medicine relied on ginger to treat virtually all ailments.

### Today

Researchers are showing increased interest in the anticancer effects of one of ginger's active components, gingenol.

## Nausea Prevention Infusion

### Ingredients for 1 cup

3 slices unpeeled ginger (¼-inch thick each)

1 cup (250 ml) water

Honey and lemon juice

- In small saucepan, combine water and ginger and bring to boil. Reduce heat and simmer for 5 minutes.
- Strain and add a touch of honey and lemon juice to reduce the spicy taste.

### Nausea Remedy

Another way to relieve nausea is to chew a piece of preserved ginger or suck on a slice of fresh ginger.

## Cold Prevention Infusion

**Ingredients for 1 cup**

3 tbsp walnuts

1 tbsp fresh onion, chopped

1 piece ginger (¾-inch thick), chopped

1 cup (250 ml) water

- In small saucepan, combine ingredients. Bring to boil and let simmer until liquid has reduced by half.
- Strain and drink hot.

## Cough Relief Infusion

**Ingredients for 2 cups**

1 piece ginger (1-inch thick), grated

½ lemon, sliced

1 clove

2 cups (500 ml) boiling water

Juice of ½ lemon

- In a small teapot, combine ginger, lemon slices, and clove.
- Pour boiling water, cover, and infuse for 10 minutes.
- Strain, add lemon juice, and drink hot.

## Cold Treatment Infusion

**Ingredients for 2 cups**

2 sticks cinnamon

¼ tsp nutmeg

1 piece ginger (1-inch thick), grated

1 clove

2 cups (500 ml) boiling water

A few drops honey

- Put cinnamon, nutmeg, ginger, and clove in the bottom of a small teapot.
- Pour in boiling water and infuse for 10 minutes.
- Strain and drink hot.

## Heartburn Relief Infusion

1 handful fresh mint leaves

1 handful fresh lemon balm leaves

4 slices unpeeled ginger ¼ inch thick each)

1 cup (250 ml) boiling water

- Combine ingredients in a small saucepan. Cover and bring to boil.
- Reduce heat and let simmer, uncovered, for 10 minutes.
- Strain and drink.

# Laurel or Bay Leaves

The bay laurel, also known as the true laurel and the Grecian laurel, is the only comestible laurel leaf. The plant family Lauraceae is comprised of evergreen trees and shrubs that are often very aromatic. The bay laurel tree is dioecious, meaning that each one carries only one sex of flower. It has bushy green foliage and yields small black berries.

A crown of laurel leaves was a mark of the highest distinction in Ancient Greece. In the Middle Ages, students who passed their exams received a crown of laurels and the title of laureate—*baccalauréat*, the French word for bachelor's degree, literally means laurel berry (*bacca laurea*). Dedicated to Apollo, the tree was once venerated by both the Greeks and Romans who saw it as an emblem of victory: like the olive tree, it could serve no profane purpose, and was never burned on altars. In Christianity, it is considered a beneficial plant that is blessed on Palm Sunday. It was even thought to be a magic plant because it crackled when eaten, even when green.

When crinkled, the leaves emit a strong aromatic odor reminiscent of eucalyptus and cinnamon. The laurel berry is rich in essential oil and is similar to the oil contained in the leaves. A typically European spice, it is never used in Asian cuisine except occasionally in the Philippines due to the country's Spanish influence.

## Therapeutic Properties

Laurel oil is antirheumatic and a concoction made with the plant's root can be taken as an expectorant. The fruit is used to treat jaundice when taken internally and rheumatic ailments when used externally.

### Antibacterial

The laurel leaf is actively antibacterial, antiviral, and bactericidal. Because of these properties, it is an effective remedy for cuts, canker sores, and dental abscesses. The oil extracted from its fruit is a formidable tool against insects and parasites, lice and mites. Aleppo soap, fabricated since its invention thousands of years ago in ancient Mesopotamia, is made with olive oil and 20% laurel oil. It is frequently recommended by dermatologists to fight acne, eczema and psoriasis.

### Flu and Lung Infections

Laurel's stimulating and warming effects are highly useful in cases of bronchitis, laryngitis, pharyngitis, flu, and chills. It is also used as a pulmonary antiseptic and as an expectorant to treat colds and bronchitis. Ground leaves are antipyretic, meaning that they reduce fever. Laurel leaves are part of theriac concoctions, which are known to ward off diseases and epidemics.

## Joint Pain

Laurel is a well-known treatment for rheumatic problems because of its diuretic and antirheumatic properties. The ripe laurel fruit produces green, fatty oil that is a common ingredient in ointments and analgesic emulsions used to treat arthritis, neuritis, and rheumatic and muscular pain.

## Digestion

The laurel leaf is a potent digestive stimulant, used successfully in the treatment of slow digestion, dyspepsia, bloating and gastroenteritis. It stimulates lazy stomachs, awakens the appetite and combats fermentation.

## Rheumatic Relief Massage Oil

½ cup (125 ml) bay leaves

¼ cup (60 ml) rubbing alcohol

2 cups (500 ml) olive oil

- Steep laurel leaves in rubbing alcohol for 24 hours in a tightly sealed bottle.
- Pour in a double boiler, add olive oil, and heat for 6 hours without allowing mixture to boil.
- Strain and keep in a cool place.

## Rheumatic Aid Bath

3 tbsp bay leaves

4 cups (¼ gallon) boiling water

- Pour boiling water on bay leaves and infuse for 10 to 15 minutes before adding to a hot bath.

*Delicious Recipes*

**Ratatouille Provençale**

**See page 158**

# Peppermint

Peppermint is an herbaceous perennial hybrid belonging to the *Lamiaceae* family, a cross between *Mentha aquatica* (water mint) and *Mentha spicata* (spearmint). It can reach a height of 15 to 25 inches. Its smooth stems are square in cross-section and bear symmetrical serrated leaves that are dark green on top and vary from light green to turquoise underneath. The plant's pink flowers are bunched in whorls at the top of the stem, and its strong peppery odor is its principal characteristic. The name *mentha* stems from Greek mythology.

Native to Europe, the mint plant grows around the world, from North America to Australia and Japan. It has long been known to the Hebrews, who used it to brew a sacred beverage. It has been cultivated since ancient times for its medicinal virtues, and was even discovered in an Egyptian tomb dating back to 1000 BCE. Menthol extraction has been a common practice in Japan for over 200 years. In 9th century France, Charlemagne introduced mint cultivation for its medicinal properties.

## Therapeutic Properties

Peppermint is an herb that everyone should have on hand. Its leaves contain an essential oil rich in menthol (a terpenic alcohol) and in menthol's corresponding ketone, menthone, to which mint owes its antiseptic and gastric anaesthetic properties. The leaves also contain flavonoids derived from apigenin and luteolin, which contribute to its curative properties.

### Cancer Prevention

Dried mint leaves contain tannins, silica, and flavonoids, yet also contain a wide variety of terpenic esters and bitter substances. Mint is an effective aid against bloating, burping and flatulence; it is also an antiseptic. Peppermint is believed to have chemopreventive properties in the colon as well as chemotherapeutic qualities in colon cancer treatments, with the added bonus of being a painkiller.

### Irritable Bowel Syndrome

For many years, peppermint was used to treat a wide range of abdominal pains. One study conducted by a McMaster University researcher and published by the British Medical Journal concluded that peppermint oil should be the first line of defense against irritable bowel syndrome, an affliction that affects between 5% and 20% of North Americans. Menthol relieves numerous symptoms such as stomachaches, abdominal cramps, bloating, constipation, and diarrhea.

## Antibacterial

Menthol is a common ingredient in many standard commercial products such as toothpaste, mouthwash, chewing gum, cough drops, as well as various ointments intended to alleviate muscle pain. The mint plant is recommended in dermatology for its emollient and anti-itch qualities. Peppermint is also an effective nasal decongestant for people suffering from colds. Menthol stimulates the nerves that are sensitive to cold and prevents them from reacting to painful stimuli, temporarily relieving pain and muscle and organ spasms all while providing a pleasant cooling sensation. Menthol also helps fight bacteria, fungi and certain viruses, placing it in the ranks of other essential oils such as garlic, hyssop, basil, marjoram, oregano, winter savory and three kinds of thyme, which have all demonstrated powerful antimicrobial properties. Some harmful bacteria peppermint oil is known to destroy include listeria, staphylococcus and salmonella.

## Therapeutic Uses

## Digestive Aid Tea

### Ingredients for 2 cups

1 handful fresh mint leaves

1 handful fresh lemon balm leaves

2 cups (500 ml) boiling water

- Put mint and lemon balm leaves in a teapot.
- Fill teapot with boiling water and stir.
- Infuse for 5 minutes and serve.

## Fresh Breath Mouthwash

2 sprigs fresh mint

2 cups (500 ml) boiling water

- Pour boiling water over fresh mint and let infuse until cool.
- Strain and use as mouthwash.

## Headache and Congestion Relief Oil

2 to 3 drops peppermint essential oil

2 tbsp canola oil

- Apply to temples and forehead and massage in a circular motion, avoiding the eye area..
- Repeat every 15 to 30 minutes if needed.

*Delicious Recipes*

Tzatziki

See page 160

# Mustard

Mustard is a cruciferous plant in the same family as cabbage, broccoli, cauliflower, Brussels sprouts, and kohlrabi. Field mustard also goes by wild mustard and charlock. Its seeds are small, varying in color between yellowish-white and black. It has been used for centuries as a spice, a recipe ingredient, and a medicinal compound. Mustard leaves are eaten in salads in certain parts of the world. Its grains contain an enzyme that is activated in cold water.

The most widely used and cultivated mustard variety is brown mustard, which has a bitter, spicy taste. The most flavorful variety is black mustard, spicier than brown mustard. White and yellow mustards are spicy and sweet.

Mustard is native to the Mediterranean Basin, China, and India. It was introduced by the Arabs, who took advantage of its medicinal properties, and by the 13th century had become a popular condiment, served as a spicy paste obtained by grinding the seeds. Dijon, France has been known as the mustard capital since the 14th century. The grains used in this famous mustard are not cultivated locally—they are shipped from Canada, the world's number one exporter of mustard.

## Therapeutic Properties

Mustard poultices have long been used as a bronchial decongestant. Mustard grain infusion foot baths have been known to relieve sore feet.

### Cancer Prevention

Brown mustard seeds found in both Dijon and English mustard contain many compounds that curb the development of cancer. Yellow mustard seeds contain ten times more antioxidants than prepared mustard, though the latter still has a place on the list of the fifty foods with the highest antioxidant content per 3 ½ ounces. Mustard seeds are also a source of selenium, a mineral that prevents the development of free radicals.

## Therapeutic Uses

### In History

16th century seafarers chewed mustard seeds in order to ward off scurvy; 17th and 18th century physicians used it to induce vomiting.

### Today

Mustard seeds are in eighth place on the list of most effective antioxidant foods, and studies are currently being conducted to better evaluate their ability to fight cancer, cardiovascular diseases, and illnesses linked to aging.

## Digestive Aid Infusion

1 tbsp mustard seeds

1 cup (250 ml) boiling water

- Pour boiling water on mustard seeds, infuse for 15 minutes, strain.

Gargle with infusion to soothe sore throats and relieve the pain of toothaches.

## Stimulating Chill Relief Bath

½ cup (125 ml) mustard powder

1 cup (250 ml) cold water

- Combine mustard and cold water and make a liquid paste. Add water if needed.
- Add to bath water.

## Cold and Bronchitis Relief Poultice

1 tbsp dried mustard

4 tbsp flour

Warm water

- In a bowl, sift together mustard and flour.
- Add enough water to make a paste.
- Spread paste on a piece of muslin large enough to cover the chest, then cover with another piece of muslin.
- Place poultice on the chest for around 12 minutes. As soon as the skin begins to redden, remove poultice. Do not leave poultice on for more than 30 minutes.
- Spread a layer of Vaseline on the chest to help preserve heat.

*Delicious Recipes*

**Rabbit with Two-Mustard Sauce**

**See page 162**

# Nutmeg and Mace

Nutmeg is a product of the nutmeg tree, in the *Myristicaceae* family. It is a bushy tree with light yellow apricot-like fruit streaked with green and red markings. Ancient naturalist Pliny the Elder spoke of a tree from which not one, but two spices could be extracted, and he was most likely describing the nutmeg tree, which bears both nutmeg and mace. Mace exudes an odor of cinnamon and pepper, with a less peppery and strong taste than nutmeg's, which has a warm and spicy flavor. Inside the fruit is a brown nut, nearly round, dense, oily and hard, wrapped in a thin woody membrane called an aril (the mace flower). Mace is the nutmeg seed's husk. This fleshy skin is comprised of lacy fibers, and the color of these fibers indicate the tree's origin: bright scarlet, brown, and reddish-orange flowers come from Indonesia; if they are light, yellowy-orange or beige, they are native to Grenada.

The aril, more commonly known as mace, turns yellowy-brown once dried in the sun, before being sold in strips, small pieces or in powder. The pit is dried in the sun until the nut inside produces a rattling sound. This takes up to one to two months; the nut is then dipped in a lime-based solution. The tradition of whitewashing nutmeg originates in Holland: anyone caught with an untreated nut was put to the sword. For many years, nutmeg was the most expensive of all oriental spices.

Indigenous to the Moluccas archipelago in Indonesia, the nutmeg tree is an evergreen that grows on tropical islands. It is now cultivated in Indonesia, Malaysia, Sri Lanka, Sumatra, and in the Leeward Antilles.

## Aphrodisiac and Hallucinogenic

Nutmeg has long been considered an aphrodisiac: it was one of the main ingredients in love potions up until the early 20th century. Some phytotherapists still prepare aphrodisiacs by combining nutmeg decoctions with cinnamon decoctions. Various powerful alkaloids, myristicin (highly toxic), safrol, and elemicin, can be found in nutmeg, and in small doses (from 1 tsp), it becomes a veritable drug capable of causing hallucinations, delirium, and even fainting.

## Therapeutic Properties

### In History

Slaves on 16th century merchant boats traveling towards Europe would use nutmeg as a sedative in order to soothe their pain and fatigue, though it was a risky remedy, as the side effects could be overwhelming, were long-lasting, and could cause death.

### Today

Nutmeg is sometimes recommended as a general or intestinal antiseptic in cases of digestive issues, and as a circulatory and nervous system stimulant. It also has emmenagogic properties (it stimulates menstrual blood flow) and could help dissolve gallbladder stones. Taken in combination with clove and rosemary essential oils, nutmeg's essential oil is a suitable dental analgesic. It is sometimes used against rheumatic pain.

## Digestive Aid Infusion

**Ingredients for 1 cup**

8 fresh mint leaves

1 pinch nutmeg

1 cup (250 ml) boiling water

- Place mint leaves and nutmeg in a teapot.
- Fill teapot with boiling water and infuse for 8 minutes.

Drink 3 cups a day after meals.

*Delicious Recipes*

Cauliflower Gratin

See page 164

# Oregano

Oregano is a perennial plant in the mint family (*Lamiaceae*) Its oval petioled leaves are arranged in a cross, lightly serrated, and scattered with glandular spots. This plant thrives in a warm climate, where its buds bloom into violet, pink, and sometimes white flowers. Oregano exudes an aroma resembling that of thyme. Its extracted essential oil is camphorated, sweet, warm, and slightly spicy, and contains carvacrol and thymol, both phenols with antibacterial, antifungal, anti-infective, antispasmodic, and energizing properties. Oregano is used fresh or dried.

This plant is native to North Europe. *Origanum vulgare* grows on the European continent, whereas *Origanum heracleoticum* grows in Italy. Marjoram, or *Origanum majorana*, is a close cousin to the *vulgare* species and is native to North Africa and Southwest Asia; it goes by the name sweet marjoram or knotted marjoram. These two species differ in odor given that oregano's scent comes from the thymol it contains (as does thyme's) and its carvacrol, whereas marjoram does not contain these phenols. In its wild state, oregano can be found in sunny areas, in bushes, coniferous and oak forests, and along the edge of rivers.

## Therapeutic Properties

The red elixir obtained by infusing oregano's flowers and leaves is known to relieve coughs, flu, indigestion, and painful menstrual cramps. When inhaled, oregano treats bronchitis and asthma. Used as a compress or as an essential oil, it soothes the pain of cramps and arthritis. Plants in the *Lamiaceae* family boast notable antioxidant activity due to the essential oils' phenols. Oregano's principle active ingredient is rosmarinic acid, but other phenolic compounds such as apigenin, luteolin, and carnosic acid could also be responsible for the herb's antioxidant effect. Oregano also contains quinic acid and kaempferol, other renowned antioxidants that slow down the biochemical deterioration of human cells. Fresh oregano provides antioxidant activity forty times more potent than that of apples, twelve times that of oranges, and four times that of blueberries.

### Cancer
The phenols thymol and carvacrol have the ability to protect the system and cells against the devastating effects of stress that cause aging, degenerative diseases, and cancers.

### Diabetes
Thanks to its antioxidant property, oregano's rosmarinic acid is thought to contribute in part to inhibiting an enzyme that increases blood sugar levels.

## Antiseptic

Oregano is a good antiseptic for the respiratory tract. Its various components (thymol, terpene, linalol, ocimene) endow it with various healing properties. Like other medicinal plants, oregano is a primary ingredient in the fabrication of numerous pharmaceutical remedies. Thanks to its expectorant and antispasmodic properties, it is a common component of cough suppressing teas. It effectively stimulates the appetite and relieves gastric and biliary troubles. Infusing one teaspoon per cup of water helps alleviate nervous fatigue, overall weakness, and sexual disorders. Oregano is also used to treat rheumatism, against chills, fever, and in some cases of gastrointestinal ailments.

## Antifungal

Numerous studies have shown that oil of oregano and its most active components, carvacrol and thymol, destroy a vast array of bacteria and fungi. Carvacrol is used as a disinfectant and antimycotic, whereas thymol is known as an antimicrobial substance and is used in disinfectants, analgesic products, and mouthwashes.

## Blood Sugar Reduction Tea

### Ingredients for 4 cups

1 tbsp dried oregano leaves
4 cups (¼ gallon) boiling water

- Pour boiling water over dried leaves. Infuse for 5 minutes and strain.

. . . . . . . . . . . . . . . . . . . . . . . . . . . .
### Note

Do not infuse the herb longer than 5 minutes. The dosage of 1 tablespoon of dried leaves per ¼ gallon of water should be respected. A higher concentration could provoke an adverse stimulating effect, particularly in the digestive system.

*Delicious Recipes*

Tomato Oregano Pizza

See page 166

# Parsley

Native to the southern parts of Europe, parsley is a biennial herbaceous plant in the *Apiaceae* family. The leaves of the parsley plant are most commonly used in cooking, although Central Europeans also use its taproot. It is quite aromatic and exudes a distinct odor. There are three main species of parsley. Curly leaf parsley has deep green leaves and long stems that can grow up to 1 foot. Flat leaf parsley has smooth leaves and can reach 1.5 feet in height. It has an aromatic flavor similar to celery's and is less bitter than curly leaf parsley. Root parsley or Hamburg root parsley is mostly grown for its white root resembling the salsify, and it measures around ½ foot long and 1 inch wide. It was highly valued as a seasoning during the Middle Ages thanks to Charlemagne, who championed its cultivation.

## Therapeutic Properties

Curly or flat, parsley is extremely rich in vitamins B and E; its vitamin C content surpasses that of citrus fruits, kiwis, and broccoli. Cooking makes this precious vitamin disappear, as along with its carotene (provitamin A) and its antioxidant properties. Parsley is also rich in other indispensable nutritional elements and minerals, such as potassium, calcium, magnesium, and iron. Apiol, an aromatic compound, is extracted from its essential oil. Parsley leaves are used in folk medicine as a resolvent when applied externally in a poultice to alleviate breast engorgement.

### Cancer

Apigenin, a flavonoid found in great quantities in parsley, is known chiefly for its antioxidant effects and its potentially antimutagenic and anticancer effects in animals. The effects of parsley's apigenin have not yet been directly studied. A study of subjects who consumed a ¾-ounce portion of fresh parsley over the course of a week showed that individual absorption of parsley's apigenin content varied. However, the subsequent increase of two antioxidant enzymes in the subjects' blood suggests that parsley intake could diminish the damages caused by free radicals in certain individuals.

### Diabetes

Parsley's apigenin could contribute to maintaining healthy blood sugar levels. In one study, researchers administered parsley extract to diabetic rats for several days and noticed a subsequent drop in their blood sugar levels.

### Halitosis

Parsley fights bad breath by trapping the sulfide compounds that develop in the mouth and intestine, particularly after the ingestion of garlic.

### Diuretic

Infused, parsley root is used as a diuretic and as an appetite stimulant. Parsley leaves and seeds are stimulants and emmenagogues (they encourage menstrual blood flow).

## Therapeutic Uses

### In History

Hippocrates believed parsley to be abortive, and it was used to induce abortions up until the Middle Ages.

### Today

Due to parsley's high apigenin content, researchers are looking into the role this highly antioxidant flavonoid could play against diabetes, certain cancers, cardiovascular diseases, and age-related diseases.

## Digestive Aid Tea

2 tbsp fresh parsley leaves

4 cups (¼ gallon) boiling water

- Pour boiling water over parsley leaves.
- Infuse for a few minutes.

Drink 1 cup after a rich meal.

*Delicious Recipes*

Tabbouleh

See page 170

# Chili Peppers

The pepper family comprises twenty-odd species and over three hundred varieties of plants that all produce plump pods. It includes all varieties of paprika and red peppers, but the three most important are the *Capsicum annuum*, the *Capsicum frutescens*, and the *Capsicum chinense*. *Capsicum frutescens* was one of the first plants to be cultivated in South America around 7,000 years ago. Today, India is pepper's primary producer and exporter, with a sizable portion of its harvest consumed domestically. Other producers and exporters include Thailand, Mexico, Japan, Turkey, Nigeria, Ethiopia, Uganda, Kenya, and Tanzania.

Among the most popular varieties are green peppers (*jalapeño, serrano, poblano*), yellow peppers (*carib, guero*), and purple or red peppers (*ancho, cascabel, japone, hontaka, pasilla*). Red peppers vary in shape and in size but are still part of the genus *Capsicum*. The cayenne pepper belongs to the *Solanaceae* family, is very spicy, and is most often consumed in powder form once dehydrated. It is used to season Indian curry dishes as well as chilis, chili being the Aztec word for the pepper.

## Therapeutic Properties

Peppers' greatest benefits are owed to its capsaicin, the active component responsible for their spicy flavor and the burning sensation they cause when eaten. The pain releases endorphins that create a sensation of well-being, which could explain its popularity as a flavoring and seasoning. Capsaicin is responsible for the decongestant, expectorant, warming and soothing properties of peppers. When eaten fresh, capsaicin promotes the digestion of starch, acts as a stimulant of the system and the appetite, and is stomatic and rubific (reddens the skin). The flavor of peppers mainly comes chiefly from its essential oils, whereas their color comes from the various carotenoids they contain, ranging from bright red (capsanthin, capsorubin) to yellow (cryptocapsin).

### Cancer

A study of several of the antioxidants contained in peppers showed their most active compound to be luteolin, followed by capsaicin, then quercetin. Hot peppers also contain many flavonoids. Some varieties are good sources of alpha-tocopherol, a form of vitamin E with antioxidant properties. The hot chili pepper is an excellent source of vitamin C, iron, manganese, vitamin $B_6$, and vitamin K. The spicy capsaicin in hot peppers binds itself to the mitochondria of cancer cells and cause apoptosis, the self-engendered death of harmful cells, without damaging the system's healthy cells. Despite the fact that it causes a burning sensation it causes in the mouth, capsaicin protects against gastroduodenal ulcers (in the stomach, large intestine and oesophagus) and reduces the side effects of certain anti-inflammatory drugs.

## Diabetes

Regular intake of foods spiced with peppers is linked to lower blood sugar levels. Peppers helps the system break down insulin more efficiently. Through its action in the liver, capsaicin indirectly provokes lower insulin secretion by the pancreas. Many studies have shown a correlation between a spicy diet and an increase in energy expenditure and fat oxidization. Researchers at Laval University observed that eating a spicy appetizer reduced the total caloric intake of the meal that followed by 200 calories, and attributed this lower intake to capsaicin. They also discovered that coffee and hot pepper lowered the daily caloric intake of overweight subjects by 1,000 calories.

A Greek study recently demonstrated that capsaicin consumed in food increased the basal metabolism, increased the feeling of fullness, and decreased food intake. Consistent pepper consumption diminishes the risk of developing hyperglycemia; in a control group, researchers observed that blood sugar levels dropped by 40% because the liver had been stimulated by capsaicin, which accelerated insulin production in the pancreas.

## Rheumatic Diseases

Capsaicin is responsible for the analgesic properties of peppers. The American Food and Drug Administration approved its use in ointments and lotions intended to relieve the pain of rheumatoid and degenerative arthritis. It also stimulates the production of substance P, a neuropeptide responsible for setting off pain when the body suffers an injury. By depleting the reserves of substance P, capsaicin acts as analgesic. It does not actually cause chemical burns, it merely causes the sensation of burning.

## Caution

Capsaicin is not water-soluble, but it is fat-soluble. In order to reap its full benefits, consume it with a bit of milk, a piece of cheese, or another food containing oil or fat.

*Delicious Recipes*

**Fish Pasta Medley**

See page 174

# Allspice

Allspice is the fruit of the myrtle pepper tree and is characterized by its odor of clove, nutmeg, pepper, and cinnamon, hence its name. This tree has a tall green trunk with evergreen leaves, can grow up to 4 feets in height, and is related to the clove tree. Its small white flowers yield clusters of fruit: small round berries the size of a pea, picked green in order to keep their aroma and dried in the sun or in an oven. Dried, they are dark brown or red.

Allspice contains between 65 and 80% eugenol, and its leaves provide vanillin, the vanilla aroma. In the Caribbean, indigenous tribes have long been using this spice as a pepper. The Mayans and Aztecs recognized its many curative virtues. The Amazons use the tree's young shoots to treat burns caused by caustic latex. Allspice's curative properties are very similar to those of cloves: it is a digestive aid, a carminitive, and and antirheumatic.

## Therapeutic Properties
(see Cloves)

## Therapeutic Uses

In the Caribbean, allspice leaves are steeped in rum in order to produce bay rum, a concoction used to massage tight muscles or to decongest the respiratory tract.

## Allspice Scented Oil

### Ingredients
4 cups (¼ gallon) olive oil
1 tbsp allspice berries
2 branches fresh thyme or rosemary

### Preparation
- Crush allspice berries with mortar. Place in a bottle with thyme and pour in oil. Let steep for 1 month and then strain.

Use this oil in salads or for grilling, or in chicken or shrimp dishes. Make sure to dilute it with a neutral oil, such as rapeseed or sunflower oil.

See
page 176

# Delicious Recipes

Spiced Veal Burgers

# Black Pepper

In India in the 4th century BCE, black pepper was known as *pippali*, the Sanskrit root of the word pepper. The plant is a thick and woody flowering vine related to vanilla that grows up to 32 feet high in tropical forest environments. Its small white flowers are grouped in cylindrical spikes up to ½ foot in length. These flowers are picked, fermented for several days, and then dried in the sun. Each part of the peppercorn has its own properties. The alkaloid piperine contained in each grain is what gives pepper its spice, whereas the pericarp, or skin, gives it its distinctive aroma. Composed of essential oils, resin, and piperine, pepper is endowed with the intense flavor of its skin. The fruit darkens to become black pepper.

The pepper tree is an ancient plant that thrived in the wild in the humid and shady forests of India, namely on the Malabar Coast, and in the regions bordering the South China Sea (Indochina, Malaysia). Black pepper trees were successfully transplanted to Mauritius and Reunion Island. Only the fruit of the *Piper nigrum* and the *Piper longum* can legally be called pepper.

White pepper is obtained by leaving the fruit on the vine for a longer period of time before picking, and then soaking it to remove the flesh and the white seed at the heart of the berry. Green pepper, cultivated in India, Indonesia, Sri Lanka, Brazil, and Madagascar is the unripe fruit that has been dried and lyophilized; these peppercorns are conserved either in brine or in salt. Red pepper from Pondicherry in India is the full ripe grain of the *Piper nigrum*: its taste is full, spicy, and intense. Cubeb pepper, grown in Java and Sumatra, is also known as tailed pepper: its fruit are smaller than *Piper nigrum*, and its aroma is fine, fresh, and potent.

Long pepper, sometimes called Indian long pepper, is cultivated in India and Borneo and grows wild in the foothills of the Himalayas, where it is harvested before ripening and dried in the sun. This variety of pepper was treasured in ancient times; the Greeks revered it and the Romans valued it at three times the price of black pepper. It was also used in medieval European cuisine. Renowned for its digestive properties, it was prescribed for bloating and liver disorders. Today, long pepper is regaining its former popularity. High-end grocers and specialized spice stores stock it on their shelves alongside other rare spices. It is used whole, and its flavor is warm, spicy, and slightly sweet. It contains more piperine than black pepper.

# Therapeutic Properties

Piperine has antimicrobial, anti-inflammatory, hepatoprotective, and antimutagenic properties. Furthermore, it promotes the absorption and bioavailability of numerous substances in the system, such as vitamins, minerals, medications and polyphenols.

## Cancer

Pepper's piperine improves the body's absorption of other dietary elements: the prized turmeric, beta carotene (precursor to vitamin A), selenium, and epigallocatechin (EGCG), green tea's well-known anticancer antioxidant. It therefore plays a role in preventing cancer. Indian cuisine usually combines pepper with turmeric. Recent scientific work has illustrated the determining role played by piperine in protecting cells against inflammation. It has been proven that encouraging turmeric absorption protects cells, which inhibits the entry of toxins and prevents them from degenerating. Cellular inflammation is known to happen before cellular degeneration and the beginning stages of cancer.

## Skin Disease

Black pepper could help treat serious skin problems, which affect roughly 1% of the population. Vitiligo destroys the skin's melanin and causes it to lose its pigmentation. Because melanin protects against the sun's damaging ultraviolet rays, people who suffer from vitiligo are more susceptible to skin cancer. Studies have shown piperine to be effective in preventing melanin loss when combined with ultraviolet radiation phototherapy. Researchers at King's College in London found that a targeted piperine treatment stimulated skin pigmentation, leading them to look into the use of piperine and its derivatives in treating vitiligo, which is particularly problematic in populations with darker skin. Many people afflicted with this problem do not react to hormone treatments and phototherapy, leading to an increased risk of cancer. Used on its own, piperine has been shown to even out pigmentation within six weeks.

## Cough

In traditional ayurvedic medicine, black pepper is used to treat as coughs and asthma. It is ground into a powder and brewed with clarified butter or ghee, honey, and sugar.

## Other Diseases

Pepper could help treat certain heart and urinary diseases (as a urination stimulant), digestive problems (as an enzyme stimulant), hemorrhoids, and dental and muscular pain.

# Black Pepper

## Therapeutic Uses

### Cough Suppressing Syrup

**Ingredients for 1 cup**

3 long pepper catkins

2 cups (500 ml) sugar

1 cup (250 ml) water

Juice of ½ lemon

- Drop pepper into water, bring to a boil, and infuse, boiling, for 5 minutes.
- Take saucepan off heat and cover until fully cooled.
- Strain with a coffee filter.
- Put lemon juice and sugar into a saucepan.
- Gently heat for 5 minutes until sugar is dissolved.
- Submerge saucepan in cold water to stop cooking and pour into a bottle.
- Only seal once mixture is cooled completely.

Use this syrup to sweeten tea and to calm coughs.

### Anticancer Sauce

¼ tsp ground black pepper

1 tsp turmeric

1 tbsp olive oil

- In a small bowl, combine ingredients and mix well.

Add to dishes during cooking.

Turmeric is one of the most recommended anticancer foods and the body absorbs turmeric 1,000 times more effectively when combined with pepper, which only increases its powerful healing effects. Add the following seasoning to vegetables, stews, fish, sauces, salads, soups, rice, pasta, etc.

# Pink Pepper

The spice known as pink pepper is actually a pink berry and can be found on supermarket shelves as Brazilian pepper, rose pepper, and Christmasberry. It is the fruit of a weeping evergreen shrub, or *Schinus terebinthifolius*, that can grow up to 50 feet high. The tree is found mainly between Mexico and Argentina, though it grows and can spread rapidly in all warm climates, including South America and Reunion Island. A close relative of the cashew tree in the *Anacardiaceae* family along with mango and sumac, this plant's evergreen leaves are aromatic, exuding an odor of pepper and turpentine. Once ripe, the fruit is picked and dried. The berries possess an aromatic flavor, sweet at first, then becoming warm and almost peppery on the tongue. They are often found mixed with black, green, and white pepper, as well as with allspice. Native Americans commonly used the entire tree. It is known to have therapeutic uses, but is mostly used for the flavor it brings to dishes and in the popular four-pepper blend.

## Delicious Recipes

**Pepper-Crusted Filet Mignon**

See page 180

# Licorice

Native to Southern Europe and Asia, licorice is a perennial plant with aromatic roots. Its name designates both the medicinally used root and the candy and is the result of a linguistic deformation of the Latin *licorece*, which is also the root of the word liquor. Its scientific name *Glycyrrhizza* comes from the Greek *glucus* (sweet) and *rhiza* (root). Licorice was known to the Greeks and Romans, from Theophrastus to Hildegard of Bingen, who used it to warm up the voice.

This medicinal plant's leaves are a lovely tender green, and its clustered flowers are blue or purple. The roots, more precisely the underground stems called stolons, are the most commonly used part of the plant.

Children across the globe enjoy chewing the sweet licorice stick as a treat. Licorice sticks contain very active elements: coumarins, flavonoids, and saponins, which contain glycyrrhizin, famous for its hepatic, expectorant, respiratory and anti-inflammatory properties. Glycyrrhizin has one negative property: it causes hypertension and can provoke edema.

## Therapeutic Properties

### Cancer

Several teams of American researchers have observed that a specific molecule extracted from licorice can halt the growth of breast and prostate cancers by deactivating a protein that feeds cancer cells. Licochalcone-A was tested *in vitro* on the tumor cells of patients suffering from prostate, breast, or blood cancers, and all cells were destroyed. One particular brand of licorice tea is labeled as anticancer tea in the United States. Other studies have drawn a link between licorice and cell apoptosis in cancer cells. These results confirm what the Chinese have known for hundreds of years, and the licorice root, which stimulates the Qi (life energy), is still widely used in many Chinese anticancer remedies.

### Cholesterol

A recent study has shown that a very small amount of licorice extract lowers cholesterol and related blood lipids in patients suffering from cardiovascular problems.

### AIDS Research

American researchers eradicated the herpes virus and Japanese researchers arrived at promising results in AIDS-related testing. Licorice's glycyrrhizin and glycyrrhizic acid slow the virus' development and make it difficult for it to latch onto healthy cells. This effect could also prove helpful against SARS, or severe acute respiratory syndrome.

## Ulcers

Researchers conducted a two-year study of 82 people suffering from gastric ulcers and observed that licorice was just as effective as cimetidine, a drug used to treat the ailment. Licorice consumption stimulates stomach secretions, protecting it against ulcers. Every year, numerous other studies are published on licorice, which is now officially recognized by the materia medica of the European community and of the United Kingdom.

## Canker Sores

Licorice is a healing agent with anti-inflammatory properties capable of treating canker sores as well as painful and debilitating ulcerations. Regularly applying a licorice patch to the affected area helps relieve pain and accelerate healing. An oral licorice patch is now available in the United States.

# Therapeutic Uses

## In History

Long ago, licorice and couchgrass were standard ingredients in hospital-prescribed tonics and medicines.

## Today

Licorice's role as a treatment for stomach problems was further developed in the mid-20th century and has since been used to treat gastric ulcers.

## Sore Throat Remedy Tea

### Ingredients for 1 cup

6 or 7 pieces of Chinese licorice root (found in Chinese herb stores)

½ to 1 tsp tea leaves

1 cup (250 ml) water

- Put licorice root and tea leaves into a teapot.
- Boil water and pour into teapot.
- Let infuse for 5 minutes before drinking.

*Delicious Recipes*

Licorice Muffins

See page 182

# Rosemary

Rosemary's Latin name *rosmarinus* means dew of the sea. This bush in the *Lamiaceae* family has also been called the crown herb and has been a venerated plant in many cultures. Its leaves once adorned the heads of young brides and Greek students, and were well-known for their stimulating effect on mental functions.

This herb is a condiment and is also melliferous—its honey is highly prized and a common ingredient in perfume. The mature plant can reach 5 feet in height and bears tough evergreen leaves with no petiole that are long and thin, lightly curled at the edges, a deep glossy green color on top, and a whitish-green shade underneath. Rosemary's very camphorated odor is evocative of incense. Its flowers vary from light blue to violet and its fruit is brown.

Rosemary grows wild along the entire edge of the Mediterranean, especially in loam soil near lavender, thyme and sage. These four aromatic herbaceous plants perfume the air of Southern France. Other rosemary-producing countries include Spain, Morocco, and Tunisia. It is also a garden plant.

## Therapeutic Properties

Like other plants in its family, rosemary contains rosmarinic acid, which has antioxidant activity far superior to that of vitamin E. This acid inhibits the production of nitric oxide as well other reactive oxygen species and nitrogen in macrophages, preventing damages linked with oxidizing stress and cellular aging. Rosmarinic acid contributes to cell viability.

### Cancer

Rosemary contains two acids, rosmarinic acid and ursolic acid, which, once combined, endow it with powerful antioxidant action. Both have a long-term effect in the system: when they decompose, they convert to different acids, which act in a cascading effect. Rosmarinic acid is present in most plants of the *Lamiaceae* family, particularly lemon balm, sloe, basil, sage, savory, and oregano, and makes up more than 3% of the dry weight of these plants. Rosemary can be used as a preventive treatment in the early phases of cancer, as it is an excellent source of polyphenols, which are found in red wine and green tea.

Rosmarinic acid is largely responsible for the herb's anticancer effects. Rosemary triggers the production of detoxifying enzymes, which combat exogenic and endogenic toxic compounds. Some of its compounds prevent carcinogens from bonding with DNA. When added to grilled meat, it nullifies the polycyclic aromatic hydrocarbons (PAHs) and heterocyclic amines (HCAs), carcinogenic substances produced while meat is being cooked.

Another Japanese herb used in cooking, *Perilla frutescens* (known in Japan as *shiso*), has an extract rich in rosmarinic acid that has also demonstrated great anticancer potential through two separate effects: an anti-inflammatory effect by inhibiting cell adhesion molecules, and an antioxidant effect by curbing DNA damage. *Shiso* has been used in Korea as a traditional anti-inflammatory to treat allergies and allergy-related asthma. Animal and clinical testing have both confirmed these effects, particularly in rhinoconjunctivitis sufferers.

## Rheumatic Diseases

Rosemary was used long ago in poultices to treat rheumatism and to heal wounds. It relieves rheumatic pain thanks to rosmarinic acid's effect on prostaglandins derived from unsaturated lipids, increasing cellular protection and preventing inflammation. Massaging stiff joints with a few drops of rosemary oil can give them a second life!

## Therapeutic Uses

### In History
Rosemary was considered an excellent anti-aging condiment because it was believed to stimulate the intellect.

### Today
At the end of the 20th century, scientists discovered how to extract rosemary's antioxidants, which can now be used by the food industry as a preservative instead of potentially carcinogenic synthetic compounds.

*Delicious Recipes*

Greek Chicken

See page 184

# Saffron

Saffron's name is derived from the Persian word for yellow (*safra*). This flower has been prized since the age of the pharaohs, and the ancient Egyptians used it to purify their temples and holy places, as an offering to the gods, or to dye their silks. In the Orient, saffron is thought to bring joy and wisdom, and Buddhist monks used it to dye their robes. The Egyptians, Hebrews, Indians and Persians would cultivate as a spice, whereas the Romans used it particularly in tea.

Saffron is one of the world's most expensive spices. Each bulb yields one or two bright or deep violet flowers that bloom in autumn. The spice is the pistil of the crocus, extracted from the flower's stigma, which is handpicked and then dried. It takes between 100,000 and 150,000 flowers to obtain 2 ¼ pounds of dried stigmas, worth between eight hundred and two thousand dollars on the market. Saffron's aromatic qualities are exceptional, as it contains over 150 volatile and non-volatile aromatic compounds. It owes its golden-orange color to its crocin.

Native to the Middle East, it was first cultivated in Greek provinces. The current primary exporter is Kashmir, followed by Iran, Morocco, Spain, and France.

## Therapeutic Properties

Saffron contains an essential oil, safranal (around 50%), the terpenes pinene, cineol, and isophorene, and picrocrocin, which give it a more pleasant taste. It has between 5 and 25% pigments, crocetin, and crocin, its paramount pigment, which gives saffron its bright yellow to orange color depending on the pigment concentration. These carotenoids are hydrosoluble, which is extremely rare. It has one of the highest levels of riboflavin of all vegetables. Also rich in antioxidants, it helps slow the aging process by neutralizing free radicals due to its safranal and crocin content. At concentrations varying between 500 and 1000 ppm, crocin neutralizes between 50 and 65% of free radicals.

Saffron has long been known to remedy numerous ailments. Classical herbalists considered it an effective sedative and tonic, as useful to the digestive system as to the central nervous system. Whereas the pigments stimulate the appetite, safranal acts as a sedative. In general, saffron affects the nervous system. It becomes a heating agent when added to mint tea, is recommended to relieve painful periods, and when combined with honey, can soothe teething pain.

### Cancer
In some cases, the carotenoids in saffron have been shown to possess anticancer and antimutagenic properties due to its carotenoid compound dimethyl crocetin. This compound affects leukemia cells by inhibiting their DNA replication, preventing reproduction.

### Depression

Two recent clinical studies claim that saffron could effectively treat depression. A study of forty patients suffering from mild to moderate depression showed saffron to be significantly more effective in treating their symptoms than a placebo. It was just as effective as Prozac and no side effects were observed.

## Therapeutic Uses

### In History

Throughout the Middle Ages, saffron was believed to cure all kinds of ailments, from a benign cough to the more serious smallpox.

### Today

Pharmacology has recognized and demonstrated saffron's benefits, and its effects are notably positive in studies on malignant tumors.

## Period Relief Saffron Infusion

½ tsp saffron filaments

4 cups (¼ gallon) boiled water, still hot

- Put filaments in hot water and infuse for 30 minutes.
- Drink throughout the day.

This tea is recommended for intense period pain, but also to provoke and regulate periods.

*Delicious Recipes*

**Saffron Coconut Scallops**

**See page 186**

. . . . . . . . . . . . . . . . . . . . . . . . . . . .

### Caution

Saffron is a euphoriant and should be used in moderation as it can increase the heart rate.

# Savory

This close cousin of thyme in the large *Labiaceae* family is thought to be an aphrodisiac and a stimulant. These properties may stem from the Latin root of its name, *satureia*, which means satyr's herb. There are two main species: the annual summer savory, which is common in gardens, and the mountainous perennial winter savory. It was well-loved by both Greeks and Romans and used long before the arrival of black pepper and hot peppers as a flavorful condiment, and it possesses a herbaceous and lightly mentholated taste.

It is an indispensable ingredient in Provençal cuisine and is also known as donkey's pepper, though it also goes by other names depending on the region. Native to the Mediterranean basin, it is grown mostly in France, Spain, Italy, the Balkans, Ukraine, Turkey, Lebanon and Israel.

## Therapeutic Properties

Savory is rich in essential oils, mainly thymol and carvacrol, present in particularly high levels in winter savory. Its main active compound is rosmarinic acid, a phenolic acid with antioxidant properties most beneficial to the immune, circulatory and nervous systems. Its leaves encourage digestion and prevent intestinal problems. Savory has potent antibacterial, antiviral, fungicidal and antiparasitic properties, particularly effective in the lungs and bladder. Savory's phenols are responsible for its role as a tonic and immunity stimulant, making it an excellent remedy for asthenia (loss of strength) and nervous fatigue. It is one of the most tonic plants and regular consumption is thought to lengthen life.

## Therapeutic Uses

### In History
For centuries, savory tea was believed to be a sexual stimulant.

### Today
Although studies have shown savory to have anticancer effects on human liver cells, its anticancer potential has yet to be proven.

## Stomach Ache Relief Tea

**Ingredients for 1 cup**

1 tbsp dried savory

1 cup (250 ml) boiling water

- Pour boiling water over dried savory, cover, and let infuse for 10 minutes before straining.

- Drink 2 to 3 cups of this tea per day to relieve, gas, flatulence or colic, but also to prevent infection and fatigue. To treat chills, add honey.

  This infusion can be added to a foot bath to treat fungus.

  To stimulate the appetite, drink this tea 15 minutes before eating.

  For tonsillitis, a sore throat, or to freshen breath, use the infusion as a mouthwash.

  To stimulate the intellect, add 2 cups of more concentrated infusion to bathwater.

*Delicious Recipes*

**Light and Fresh Potato Salad**

See page 188

# Sage

"He who would live for aye, must eat sage in May," as the old saying goes. The name of this reputed plant is derived from the Latin *salvare*, meaning to save. Known in Arabic as camel's tongue, its oblong green leaves are covered in grey-green fuzz and exude an extremely fragrant perfume.

This shrub grows on rocky hills in southern climates. Its stems bear green leaves covered in grey-white soft, short hairs. Its magnificent lavender blue flowers grow in spikes atop the plant, bloom in summer, and can have a rosy hue. Certain varieties have a fruity odor reminiscent of pineapple or mango, whereas others have a harsher odor of rosemary or camphor, with a light, slightly bitter taste.

Sage can be found around the world, but mainly grows in Central America, where around 800 species can be found. It is believed that sage is of Syrian origin. Depending on variety and origin, it is used in cooking and traditional medicine, or as a purifying or divinatory herb, and is even used as a ritualistic hallucinogenic. In certain Native American traditions, sage is burned to chase away evil spirits in smudging ceremonies.

## Therapeutic Properties

Considered to be a cure-all in the Middle Ages, medicinal sage was used to treat many diseases. Salviol, a type of camphor found in sage oil, has a tonic effect on the heart and nerves. Certain varieties are potent drugs. The sage leaf produces tannin that has recognized astringent and antiphlogistic properties. Also found in the leaf are phosphates, glutamine, asparagine, and various mineral compounds.

The Mayans and Aztecs grew a local variety of sage, *Salvia hispanica alba*, also known as *chia*, which is the etymological root of the name of the Mexican state of Chiapas. Chia seeds were the third most cultivated source of food at the time, after corn and wheat. For a time after the collapse of the Mayan civilization, the plant could only be found in the wild. Chia has since been rediscovered and shown to be rich in polyunsaturated fatty acids, of which over 60% are omega-3 fatty acids. Because chia is a good source of omega-3s and contains no toxic compounds, it could even be preferable to soy or flax seeds as a nutritional product. It is also commercially sold as *salba*.

## Cardiovascular Disease

Sage has anti-inflammatory and antioxidant properties. It contains flavonoids, phenolic acids, and certain enzymes that endow it with the unique capacity to prevent cell damage through oxidization. It can be used to fight rheumatoid arthritis and other inflammatory diseases, such as asthma and atherosclerosis. Sage is also rich in omega-3 fatty acids, which play a significant role in lowering the risk of heart disease, diabetes and obesity. Following fifteen years of study, University of Toronto researchers concluded that 2 tablespoons a day of ground *salba* provided 100% of the daily requirement of omega-3 fatty acids and 30% of the daily recommended amount of fiber. *Salba* absorbs fourteen times its weight in water, slows both digestion and the release of sugars by the system, and creates a prolonged sensation of satiety. Eaten for breakfast, this grain reduces the daily need for appetite-stimulating sugars while also providing many essential nutrients.

## Alzheimer's

Sage could be effective in treating mild or moderate cases of Alzheimer's disease. In one study, sage extract was administered to elderly Alzheimer's patients over the course of four months and was shown to increase their cognitive abilities and diminish agitation; patients who were administered a placebo showed no improvement. The positive effects were a result of an increased transmission of neural influxes in the brain as well as a decrease in both oxidative stress and inflammatory reactions.

## Menopause

Sage contains a phytohormone with estrogenic effects, as well as other compounds such as salvione, salviol, cineol, borneol, pinene and flavonoids. The plant has particularly powerful therapeutic effects in women, as it is known to regulate estrogen, help control menstrual blood flow, and protect against hot flashes. Sage has a positive impact on menstruation by regulating the monthly cycle, relieving menstrual pain, diminishing hot flashes, and restoring energy.

*Delicious Recipes*

Sage Saltimbocca

See page 192

# Sage

## Therapeutic Uses

### In History
The Gauls believed that sage was a remedy that cured all ills.

### Today
Sage infusions are recommended to encourage healing, as well as for digestive and liver problems.

## Hot Flash Prevention Menopause Tea

### Ingredients for 1 cup
4 to 5 fresh sage leaves

1 cup (250 ml) boiling water

- In a small teapot, pour boiling water over sage and cover.
- Let steep for 10 minutes.

A 15-day treatment of 1 cup per day is recommended.

## Digestion-Stimulating Wine

### Ingredients for 4 cups
¾ cup fresh sage leaves

⅓ cup (80 ml) sugar

4 cups (1/4 gallon) red wine

- Steep sage and sugar in red wine for 7 days.

Drink a small glass before meals.

## Sore Throat Gargle

A handful (8 to 10) fresh sage leaves

4 cups (1/4 gallon) boiling water

- Boil sage for 10 minutes in boiling water.

Use as a mouthwash for gums or canker sores, as gargle for sore throats, or as a compress for ulcers and cold sores. This infusion is equally useful for treating sprains and insect bites, and for general hair care.

## Multi-Purpose Infusion

### Ingredients for 1 cup
1 cup (250 ml) boiling water

1 tsp sage, leaves and flowers

- In a teapot, pour boiling water over sage and infuse for 10 minutes.
- Strain.

Drink 3 cups a day before meals for 3 weeks to treat circulatory or nervous gastric problems. Stop treatment for 10 days, then start again.

Sage tea reduces fever, treats diabetes and colds, and controls perspiration. Is also helps relieve dysmenorrhoea and diarrhea.

# Thyme

The word thyme comes from the Greek *thumos*, meaning odor. Thyme is a very fragrant plant and, when warmed by the sun, its sprigs fill the air with a captivating aromatic perfume. The Egyptians used it to embalm their deceased, the Greeks burned it as incense in their temples, and the Romans consecrated it to Venus.

Unlike other fine herbs that are used raw, thyme needs heat to release its many properties. This evergreen shrub is native to the Mediterranean, the Balkans, and Caucasus and is part of the *Lamiaceae* family. There are over sixty species of thyme, including wild thyme and lemon thyme. It is consumed as a fresh or dried herb and has been long appreciated for its medicinal properties.

## Therapeutic Properties

Thyme is separated into several chemical groups called chemotypes that are influenced by both the climate and environment in which the plant grows and evolves. Its essential oil contains thymol and carvacrol (up to 60%), which are excellent antiseptics and vermicides.

### Cancer

The *Lamiaceae* family includes mint, thyme, marjoram, oregano, basil, and rosemary, all of which contain terpene-rich essential oils, which give the plants their individual odors. Thyme's essential oil, thymol, is a powerful antiseptic.

The greatest characteristic of terpenes is their interference in cancer development by inhibiting certain oncogenes involved in the growth of cancerous cells. When certain terpenes, namely carvacrol and thymol, are introduced to cancerous cells, they slow the growth of these cells considerably, and in certain cases even provoke apoptosis.

Lamiaceae herbs also contain ursolic acid, an anticancer molecule that targets affected cells, preventing angiogenesis and halting inflammation.

In addition to terpenes, these herbs contain luteolin, mint and thyme's most abundant flavonoid, which plays a preventative role and exhibits other anticancer properties. It protects DNA from oxidative lesions, prevents the creation of new blood vessels used by tumors to accelerate growth, and slows the spread of cancer.

### Respiratory Disease Prevention

In cases of respiratory tract diseases, bronchial engorgement, bronchial asthma, and even whooping cough, thyme has proven to be an effective remedy when administered with an equal quantity of plantain. Thyme is recommended as a respiratory decongestant and as a breath freshener. A mixture of rosemary, lavender, thyme, and cedar nut essential oils is an effective treatment for alopecia.

## Thyme Infusion

### Ingredients for 1 cup

1 cup (250 ml) water

1 tsp dried thyme leaves or 10 young fresh sprigs

- Boil water and remove from heat. Add thyme to water and let infuse for 5 minutes.

This infusion helps relieve colds by clearing the respiratory tract.

## Inhalation

- Place a bunch of fresh thyme in a bowl, pour hot water over it, and inhale the vapors while covering the head with a towel.

## Thyme Bath

16 cups (1 gallon) water

1 cup (250 ml) fresh thyme sprigs

### Preparation

- Boil water for a few minutes. Add fresh thyme, bound by string or wrapped in cheesecloth.
- Let infuse for 15 minutes.
- Prepare a hot bath and add the infusion.

Relieves bronchitis, encourages mucus expectoration, and relaxes.

*Delicious Recipes*

**Guinea Hen with Cider and Thyme**

**See page 194**

# Herbs and Spices in the Kitchen

## Herbs and Spices in the Kitchen

This section of the book is dedicated to the use of herbs and spices in the kitchen and opens with a few recipes for traditional spice mixtures from diverse culinary backgrounds that you can prepare at home. Of course, these blends and their variations can be bought at most grocery and big box stores, but all the same, it is best to make them yourself and to choose the herbs and spices based on their distinctive characteristics.

# Baharat

Baharat base mix is a traditional ingredient in Lebanese, Syrian, Egyptian, and Jordanian cuisine, and its use is widespread all the way to Ethiopia.

## Ingredients

½ tsp ground nutmeg

1 tbsp black peppercorns

1 tbsp coriander seeds

1 tbsp cumin seeds

1 tbsp cloves

1 small cinnamon stick

6 green cardamom pods

2 tbsp paprika

1 tsp ground chili pepper

## Preparation

- In a coffee grinder, grind the seeds.
- Mix well.
- Store in a hermetically sealed container in a dark, dry place.

# Berbere

This liquid Ethiopian seasoning perfumes meats and vegetable stews.

## Ingredients (makes 2 cups)

1 tsp ground ginger

½ tsp ground cardamom

½ tsp fenugreek seeds

½ tsp fresh nutmeg, grated

¼ tsp cloves, ground

⅛ tsp ground cinammon

⅛ tsp Jamaican allspice, ground

2 tbsp onions, finely chopped

1 tbsp garlic, minced

2 tbsp salt

3 tbsp dry red wine

6 tbsp paprika

2 tbsp cayenne pepper

½ tsp freshly ground pepper

1 ½ cups (375 ml) water

2 tbsp vegetable oil

## Preparation

- In a heavy-bottomed pan, toast the ginger, cardamom, coriander seeds, fenugreek, nutmeg, clove, cinnamon, and allspice over low heat for 1 minute, stirring constantly.
- Remove from heat and let cool for a few minutes.
- In a food processor, blend the onions, garlic, 1 tsp salt and wine until smooth. Do not blend too long to prevent the mixture from heating.
- In a pan, combine paprika, cayenne pepper, black pepper and remaining salt. Roast for 1 minute over very low heat, stirring constantly. Add water ¼ cup at a time, then the spice and wine mixture. Stir vigorously over very low heat for 10 minutes.
- With a spatula, transfer the mixture into a jar, stirring well. Let cool at room temperature, and then pour a dash of oil over the container.
- Cover with plastic wrap and refrigerate.
- Change the plastic wrap after each use. This Berber paste keeps for 6 months in the refrigerator.

# Chat Masala

This traditional blend is used in the north of India.

## Ingredients

1 tsp cumin seeds

½ tsp ajowan seeds (or caraway seeds)

1 tsp black peppercorns

½ tsp cayenne pepper

1 tsp dried pomegranate seeds

1 tsp black salt

1 tsp coarse salt

½ tsp ground ginger

1 to 3 mint leaves, chopped

## Preparation

- In a frying pan over medium heat, toast the cumin and ajowan (or caraway) seeds.
- Let cool, then add the pepper, cayenne pepper, pomegranate seeds, both salts, ginger, and mint, and mix in a food processor.
- Store in container in a dry, dark place.

# Classic Curry

In India, there exist thousands of different ways to prepare *garam masala*. Here is one blend that can serve as a base for infinite variations.

## Ingredients

4 dried chili peppers

2 tbsp coriander seeds

½ tsp mustard seeds

1 tsp black pepper

1 tsp fenugreek seeds

1 tsp ground ginger

1 tsp powdered turmeric

## Preparation

- In a frying pan over medium heat, toast the chili peppers, coriander, mustard, black pepper and fenugreek.
- In a coffee grinder, blend the first five ingredients, or crush with a mortar and pestle.
- Add the ginger and turmeric and mix well.
- Store in a sealed container in dry, dark place.

# Singapore Curry

Chili peppers are the star of this blend, a great companion for poultry and meats.

## Ingredients

3 or 4 dried chili peppers

6 tbsp coriander seeds

4 green cardamom pods

1 tbsp cumin seeds

1 tbsp fennel seeds

6 cloves

2 tbsp black peppercorns

¾-inch cinnamon stick

2 tbsp ground turmeric

## Preparation

- In a frying pan over medium heat, toast the chili peppers, coriander, cardamom, cumin, fennel, cloves, black pepper and cinnamon.
- Let cool and grind in a spice grinder.
- Add the turmeric and mix well.
- Store in a sealed container in a dry, dark place.

# Chinese Five-Spice

There are many variations of Chinese five-spice. This one gives pork and chicken a warm, spicy taste.

## Ingredients

1 tbsp star anise seeds

1 tsp cinnamon

1 tbsp Sichuan chili pepper

1 tsp cloves

1 tbsp fennel seeds

## Preparation

- Grind the spices in a coffee grinder or spice grinder.
- Add cardamom or dried ginger if desired.
- Store in a sealed container in a dry, dark place.

# Antillean Colombo

Colombo is the Antillean equivalent to Indian curry. It is most often used in meat and fish dishes.

## Ingredients

3 cloves garlic

2 fresh hot chili peppers

1 tsp ground coriander seeds

1 tsp ground turmeric

1 tsp ground mustard seeds

## Preparation

- In a frying pan over medium heat, toast the chili peppers, coriander, turmeric and mustard.
- Add the garlic and then grind with a mortar and pestle or in a food processor.

# Cajun Seasoning

Cajun cuisine is the traditional food of the descendants of the Acadians, the celebrated hunters and fishers of Lousiana. This mix serves primarily to flavor fish, chicken and game.

## Ingredients

1 large clove garlic, minced

½ small onion, finely chopped

1 tsp paprika

½ tsp freshly ground pepper

½ tsp ground cumin

½ tsp ground mustard seeds

½ tsp Cayenne pepper

1 tsp dried thyme

1 tsp dried oregano

1 tsp salt

## Preparation

- For immediate use, combine all the ingredients in a food processor or spice grinder.
- To prepare in advance, grind the spices and store in a jar. Don't add the garlic and onion until ready to use.

# Thai Red Curry Paste

This curry paste comes from the Malay Peninsula and is used to season beef, duck and chicken.

## Ingredients

1 tsp cumin seeds

1 tbsp coriander seeds

1 tsp black pepper

3 shallots, minced

2 garlic cloves, minced

2 citronnella stalks

5 dried chili peppers, chopped

1 tbsp galangal (available at most Asian grocery stores)

2 tsp lime zest

1 tsp paprika

## Preparation

- In a pan, toast cumin and coriander for 2 to 3 minutes.
- Let cool and mix with black pepper.
- Add the shallots, garlic and citronella to make a fine paste.
- Add the dried chili peppers and the galangal, lime zest and paprika.
- Use immediately or freeze.

# Sambal Olek

Sambals are sauces with a chili pepper base, so they are extremely hot. They are generally served in small bowls on the side to spice up dishes.

## Ingredients

4 cups (¼ gallon) water

1 cup (250 ml) chili peppers

2 tsp salt

1 tsp brown sugar

3 tbsp white vinegar

## Preparation

- Boil water in a pot and add the chili peppers.
- Boil for 5 minutes. Drain.
- Put peppers into a food processor and add add salt, sugar and vinegar.
- Pulse until mixture is creamy.
- Will keep in the refrigerator for about 10 days.

# Garlic in the Kitchen

Garlic truly is an absolutely irreplaceable ingredient. Just imagine the flavor that would be missing from our meals without garlic! It has a place of honor in all the cuisines of the world.

## Buying

Choose plump, firm bulbs, free of sprouts and stains, with the skin intact. Garlic is available in flakes, as a powder, chopped, and as a paste. However, it is best to serve garlic fresh if you wish to enjoy its full flavor and benefit from all its properties.

## Storing

Garlic does not need to be refrigerated. This is actually a good thing, because its odor is absorbed by other foods. It keeps for several months at room temperature in a dark, well-ventilated area. Garlic stalks can be braided and hung in a ventilated place, and will keep for several months. Fresh white garlic usually keeps for about six months. Garlic can be frozen as is—simply remove the exterior skin. If you wish to keep it longer, peel and finely mince garlic cloves, place them into a small jar with a lid, and cover with oil (preferably olive oil). Simply spoon out the desired amount as needed.

Garlic can also be made into a puree. Separate all the garlic cloves without removing the skin, and rinse under water. Steam for 30 minutes or boil in a saucepan. Next, peel each clove and puree with a bit of olive oil. Keep in a closed container in the fridge. To freeze garlic, take apart the bulb, wearing gloves, before chopping it in a food processor. Next, spread on a tray and place in the freezer. Once it's well frozen, break up and store in a container in the freezer.

## Caution

Raw garlic is not recommended for people who take blood thinning medicine. It can lead to a drop in blood sugar, or cause digestive troubles and allergies in other people. Additionally, allicin becomes toxic in large doses.

## Aioli

Aioli is a mayonnaise that is made with garlic instead of mustard. So, it goes well with all foods that you would usually pair with mayonnaise, including vegetables and raw fish or appetizers and crudités. Plus, it brings together two ingredients with countless health-giving properties—garlic and olive oil.

### Ingredients for 1 cup

2 egg yolks

12 garlic cloves

1 pinch of salt

1 cup (250 ml) olive oil

### Preparation

- In a food processor, combine egg yolks, crushed garlic and a pinch of salt. Slowly pour in the olive oil, whisking constantly.

- Add oil as needed to gain the desired consistency.

# Forty Clove Roast Chicken

This recipe will please garlic lovers as much as it will those who are just discovering the wonders of garlic. Because these cloves are cooked in their skin, they have a milder flavor, but are just as tasty.

## Ingredients for 4

1 whole 3 lb chicken

40 garlic cloves, unpeeled

4 sprigs fresh thyme

2 sprigs fresh rosemary

2 bay leaves

¼ cup (60 ml) olive oil

Salt and pepper to taste

4 tbsp flour diluted in ¼ cup (60 ml) water

## Preparation

- Preheat the oven to 350°F (180°C).
- Clean out the chicken, season the cavity with salt and pepper, and stuff with all of the herbs except for the bay leaves.
- Place the unpeeled garlic cloves at the bottom of a Dutch oven or covered casserole dish.
- Place the chicken in the dish, tear the bay leaves over it and drizzle with olive oil.
- In a small bowl, mix the flour with a bit of water to make a very thick paste, which will be used to seal the cover of the casserole or Dutch oven.
- Generously spread the paste around the lid with your fingers. It will wash off easily once the chicken is cooked..
- Cook in the oven for 1 ½ hours without unsealing the cover. The garlic cloves in their sleeves make a flavorful accompaniment.

# Dill
# in the Kitchen

Dill's slight minty flavor is milder than fennel and marries beautifully with fish, especially salmon, which it seasons with finesse. It's also an absolutely delectable addition to soups, stews, and creamy sauces.

## Buying and Storing

Dill is great fresh, but it freezes very well. Its flowered tips and fresh leaves have a unique taste and appearance. Fresh dill lasts about two days, as long as its stalks are placed in a bowl of water or its leaves are kept wrapped in a wet paper towel and it is stored in the refrigerator. Store dried seeds in a sealed container in a dark, cool and dry place.

## Caution

The essential oil of dill, rich in carvone, can provoke serious anxiety problems. However, it is safe to use dill leaves and fruits in condiments.

# Salmon Gravlax with Dill

Seeing how popular sushi, sashimi and maki have become over the last few years, fans of these delicacies are starting to get creative with raw fish in their very own kitchens. Scandinavians have another way of serving raw salmon, which is certainly just as tasty as sushi.

## Ingredients for 4

1 lb fresh salmon

4 tbsp sea salt

3 tbsp sugar

1 tbsp freshly ground pepper

1 large bunch of dill (for the marinade)

1 small bunch of dill, for garnish

## Preparation

• Wash the salmon under cold water and pat dry.

• In a bowl, mix the sugar, salt, and pepper, and pour over the salmon and completely cover the salmon in the mixture.

• Wrap the dill around the salmon and cover it with plastic wrap so that the dill sticks to the fish.

• Cover with a weight and place in a dish in the refrigerator for 2 to 6 days.

• For the first 3 days, remove water from the dish every 8 to 12 hours. The fish "cooks" in this marinade and will turn an orange color.

• Just before serving, delicately clean the fish in cold water, dry it with a clean cloth, and thinly slice.

• Decorate with fresh dill leaves and serve with aioli or plain mayonnaise.

# Anise
# in the Kitchen

This wonderfully flavorful seed is often used in baking and pastries, but it also brings its distinct aroma to game, marinades and some fish dishes.

## Buying and Storing

Most often ground in a mortar, anise fruits are used in infusions and in liqueurs. Store the seeds (diakenes) in a dry, dark place. The fruit is the only part of the plant used in cooking or therapeutically.

## Caution

Green anise has no known toxicity, but never consume the pure essential oil without a prescription (toxic risk). The plant is also not recommended for children under 6 years of age or for pregnant and breastfeeding women. It is also not advised for people allergic to anethol.

# Aniseed Nut Cake

Almonds and hazelnuts are combined with rich, warm spices in this surprisingly aromatic cake.

## Ingredients

½ cup (125 ml) 15% cooking cream
¾ cup (180 ml) honey
1 tbsp aniseeds
1 pinch of cinnamon
1 tsp ground cloves
1 tsp ground juniper berries
1 tsp ground ginger
½ tsp Sichuan chili peppers, ground
½ tsp ground cardamom
Zest of 1 orange
1 egg, beaten
1 cup (250 ml) flour
1 tsp salt
1 tbsp baking powder
¾ cup (180 ml) hazelnut powder
¾ cup (180 ml) almond powder

## Preparation

- Boil the cream with the honey, add the spices and blend with a mixer.
- Cover and set aside.
- In a bowl, combine the flour, salt, baking powder, hazelnut powder and almond powder. Mix well.
- Strain the chilled cream and add to the flour mixture along with the egg. Mix well with a spatula.
- Pour the batter into a buttered cake tin and let rest at room temperature for a few minutes.
- Preheat the oven to 350°F (180°C ) and cook for 40 minutes.
- Once cooked, remove the cake from the tin and place on a cooling rack.
- Once cool, wrap the cake in plastic wrap. This cake will keep for several days.

# Star Anise in the Kitchen

Star anise's warm, fragrant taste pairs perfectly with stocks, Asian soups, pork, and duck.

## Buying and Storing

Star anise keeps very well as long as the star stays whole, while powdered star anise will lose its aroma very quickly. It is best to reduce the spice to a powder at home in small quantities and to smell it before buying it, and only buy a few stars at a time. Star anise is used whole, crushed, pulverized, ground, and distilled in baking, pastries and candy. It's one of the main spices in Chinese five-spice, which is often found in Asian dishes.

### Caution

Star anise from Japan (*Illicium religiosum*) is toxic.

## Mango Star Anise Cream

A refined and light dessert with a subtle hint of anise that also allows us to benefit from the health properties of mango, a fruit rich in carotenoids and soluble fibers.

### Ingredients for 2

1 mango

1 ½ cups (375 ml) yogurt

2 tbsp ricotta cheese

2 tbsp honey

Juice of ½ lime

The seeds of 1 star anise

1 pinch nutmeg

2 ground cherries, for garnish

### Preparation

- In a bowl, combine the peeled, chopped mango (reserving some to decorate), yogurt, ricotta, honey, lime juice, and star anise seeds.

- Puree in a blender or food processor and add nutmeg.

- Pour into cups, cover with plastic wrap and chill for at least 2 hours.

- Before serving, garnish with diced mango and ground cherries, petals open.

# Basil in the Kitchen

The incomparable scent of basil marries well with tomato, and the two are commonly combined in Italian cuisine. This herb is also the main ingredient in classic green pesto.

## Buying and Storing

Basil is best used raw because cooking decreases its fragrance. Look for fresh, brightly-colored leaves that have a robust odor, and avoid brown-tinged or wilted leaves. Dried basil can be bought chopped or ground, but it is less fragrant than fresh basil. Store dried herbs in a dark, dry place in a watertight container. To dry it, place fresh basil in a dark, well-ventilated area for several days, until the leaves become dry and crisp. It can also be spread over paper towels and dried in the microwave for two minutes on high. Throw out any leaves that turn black. To store fresh basil, loosely wrap the leaves in plastic wrap and place the stalks in a glass of water in the refrigerator for up to five days. To freeze, finely chop and put in ice cube moulds with a bit of water. Simply add a "basil ice cube" to cooked dishes, or make a pesto and freeze it in the same way to add to sauces as needed.

## Basil Pesto

In traditional pesto recipes, the leaves aren't blended but rather ground with a mortar and pestle. However, using a food processor to make pesto has become standard, as it is more practical and much quicker.

### Ingredients

1 large bunch of fresh basil leaves, rinsed and roughly chopped

3 garlic cloves, peeled and sliced

½ cup (125 ml) olive oil

4 tbsp grated Parmesan

4 tbsp pine nuts, toasted

Salt and pepper to taste

### Preparation

- In a food processor, combine the basil leaves and garlic cloves. Pour in half the oil and pulse.
- Add the Parmesan and pine nuts (toasted in a pan or in the oven) and the rest of the oil, and pulse again until a smooth texture is obtained.
- Pour into a jar and use within 2 or 3 days.
- Serve with pasta, poultry or fish.

# Cinnamon in the Kitchen

In the West we use cinnamon mostly in baking, but Asian and Maghreb cuisine has long been adding it to savory dishes, and this cooking practice is becoming more and more popular in North American cuisine.

## Buying and Storing

Cinammon is generally bought as a powder or an extract, but it is also sold in sticks. Like most spices, it needs to be stored somewhere cool, dry and dark. While ground cinnamon has the most pronounced fragrance, it also loses flavor the most quickly. To avoid this, store cinnamon in a sealed container.

## Caution

- Coumarin, one of cinnamon's compounds, can be harmful in large doses, and cinnamon oil is particularly rich in coumarin.
- Certain cinnamon supplements can interact poorly with medicines.

## Spiced Fruit Compote

An excellent winter dessert, this compote is a great source of fiber and provides energy, and also protects against cardiovascular problems.

### Ingredients

1 cup (250 ml) dried apricots

¾ cup (180 ml) dried figs

½ cup (125 ml) raisins

¼ cup (60 ml) dried apples

¼ cup (60 ml) packed brown sugar

½ cup (125 ml) melted butter or non-hydrgenated margarine

⅛ cup (30 ml) dark rum

1 tsp grated lemon zest

1 tsp lemon juice

1 tsp cinnamon

### Preparation

- In a saucepan, cover the apricots, figs, raisins and apples with water.
- Bring to a boil over medium heat and simmer, covered, for 15 minutes.
- Drain the rehydrated fruit, let cool, and chop.
- Return the fruit to the saucepan and add the other ingredients.
- Bring to a boil over medium heat and simmer, covered, for another 15 minutes.
- Serve over frozen yogurt.

# Warm Quinoa with Cranberries and Cashews

In this recipe, cinnamon is added to quinoa, a food with countless curative virtues. Little known until recently, it is one of the rare grains to contain eight essential amino acids. Seasoned with spices and orange, this dish makes a delectable light meal or a very nutritious accompaniment.

## Ingredients for four

1 cup quinoa, carefully rinsed and drained

2 cups (250 ml) water

½ tsp salt

1 tbsp dried basil

½ tsp chili powder

½ tsp cinnamon

1 tsp grated orange zest

¼ cup dried cranberries

¼ cup cashew nuts, toasted and roughly chopped

## Preparation

- Cook the quinoa in boiling salted water following the package directions. Normally, it is left to simmer for 10 minutes, uncovered, until the grains become translucent, and then removed from the heat, covered, and left to soak up remaining water for 5 minutes.

- Stir in the basil, chili powder, cinammon, orange zest, cranberries and nuts.

- Taste, adjust the seasoning, and serve lukewarm or reheated.

# Cinnamon
## in the Kitchen

## Chocolate Cinnamon Spice Cake

This light cake, flavored with cocoa and seasoned with spices, is made without eggs, butter or milk.

### Ingredients for 6 or more

1 cup (250 ml) unbleached flour

½ cup (125 ml) whole wheat flour

⅛ cup (30 ml) sugar

3 tbsp cocoa powder

1 tsp baking powder

1 tsp baking soda

1 tsp cinnamon

¼ tsp turmeric

¼ tsp pepper

¼ cup canola oil

1 cup (250 ml) water

1 tbsp lemon juice

¼ cup (60 ml) chocolate chips

### Preparation

- Preheat the oven to 350°F (180°C).
- In a large bowl, combine the flours, sugar, cocoa, baking powder, baking soda, cinnamon, turmeric and pepper.
- In a smaller bowl, mix the liquid ingredients—oil, water, lemon juice—and pour over the dry ingredients.
- Add the chocolate chips and mix well with a spatula until batter is smooth.
- Pour into a greased 8-inch square metal baking pan.
- Place in the oven and cook for 30 to 35 minutes until a toothpick inserted into the batter comes out clean and dry.
- Let cool and then decorate with the icing of your choice.

# Cardamom in the Kitchen

Cardamom seeds are an essential ingredient in curries and *garam masala*, and they are a seasoning for many, many Indian dishes. It's also often added to English pastries.

## Buying and Storing

Cardamom is sold in pods or ground, but it's best bought whole in order to conserve its flavour. Don't open the pods until ready to use, and keep somewhere dry and dark, for at the most one year for powder and two or more years for pods. It's one of the most expensive spices, along with saffron and vanilla.

## *Indian Chicken with Pistachios*

This recipe is prepared following traditional Indian methods. First, the dry spices are toasted in a pan, and then a liquid is added to create a sauce. It's a very healthy way of cooking that maintains the flavor of the spices.

### Ingredients for 4

1 whole 3 lb chicken, cut into pieces and skin removed

½ cup (125 ml) unsalted pistachios, shelled

½ cup (125 ml) coconut

1 tsp cumin seeds

1 tsp coriander seeds

4 cardamom pods, seeds removed from shells

6 Four Spice seeds

¼ tsp ground cinnamon

4 dried chili peppers in their skins

5 garlic cloves, peeled and halved

1 tbsp canola or grapeseed oil

4 cups (¼ gallon) water

Fresh cilantro leaves and finely ground pepper for garnish

### Preparation

- Heat a heavy saucepan over medium heat and toast half the pistachios, the coconut, coriander seeds, cumin, cardamom and Four Spice, cinnamon, dried chili peppers and garlic cloves for 15 minutes, stirring often to prevent the garlic from burning and reducing the heat as needed. The mix should turn a nice caramel color and will become very fragrant.

- Turn off the heat and let cool.

- Next, put this blend into a food processor with ½ cup water and pulse. Add another ½ cup of water and continue to mix until smooth.

- Transfer to a saucepan with the oil and the remaining water, reheat and drop the chicken pieces into the sauce.

- Cover, bring to a boil, reduce heat and let simmer over very low heat for 20 to 30 minutes, or until the chicken is cooked.

- Serve with cilantro, colored pepper, and the remaining pistachios.

# Curry Powder in the Kitchen

Curry powder isn't one single spice, but a blend of different herbs and spices also known as *garam masala* in India, and its ingredients vary greatly by region. The Colombo, the Sinhalese little brother of curry, is a creole version invented by Sri Lankan slaves. When they arrived in the Antilles, they introduced their own culinary traditions, which were then adopted by locals into their own cuisine.

## Buying and Storing

Like all blended spices, curry powder should be kept in a dark, dry place. Because it quickly loses flavor, it's better prepared in small batches.

## Colombo Lamb

Colombo powder, like curry powder, gives its name to dishes that contain it. The blend in this recipe goes particularly well with lamb.

### Ingredients for 4

2 lb boneless lamb shoulder, cubed

Salt and pepper to taste

1 tsp Espelette pepper

3 garlic cloves, crushed

½ tsp thyme

3 bay leaves

Juice of 4 lemons

2 onions, chopped

½ tsp mustard seeds

½ tsp coriander

½ tsp fenugreek

½ tsp cloves

½ tsp pepper

½ tsp ginger

2 tbsp turmeric

½ tsp cumin

Poultry stock or water

1 apple, peeled and diced

1 tbsp olive oil

### Preparation

- Place the cubes of lamb in a shallow dish and season them with salt and pepper, Espelette pepper, garlic, thyme and bay leaf. Add lemon juice and let marinate in the refrigerator for at least 1 hour for a maximum of 4 hours.

- While the lamb is marinating, toast all the seeds (mustard, coriander, fenugreek, cloves) in a dry saucepan, grind them and add to the other ground spices (pepper, ginger, turmeric and cumin).

- Place the marinated cubes in a Dutch oven and let them render their juices for 10 minutes. Add the chopped onions and spice blend (colombo).

- Remove the chili pepper from the marinade and pour over the meat and pour in stock or water, just until the meat is covered.

- Cover, bring to a boil, reduce heat and let simmer gently for 45 to 50 minutes.

- Add the apple 10 minutes before the lamb has finished cooking. Serve with basmati rice.

# Caraway
# in the Kitchen

Caraway is found in many traditional European dishes, including Hungarian goulash, Irish stew, potato salads and German coleslaw, as well as in baked goods like pumpernickel and Alsatian gingerbread.

## Buying and Storing

Caraway is recognizable by its brown color and the long shape of its streaked seed, curved in a half-moon. Store it in a sealed jar in a dark, dry place. Those allergic to Apiaceaes (fennel, celery) should avoid caraway.

## Caution

Caraway essential oil is toxic when taken in a large dose (toxic to nervous and renal systems). The plant is easily confused with other mortally toxic plants (such as hemolock).

## Carrot and Caraway Spread

This carrot puree is a delicious way to benefit from the properties of both of these foods: carrot helps with digestion, and caraway has tonic and antianemic properties.

### Ingredients for 4

4 large carrots

1 tsp whole caraway seeds, soaked in 1 cup (250 ml) water overnight

3 garlic cloves, minced

Chili sauce, cayenne pepper or chili pepper, to taste

4 tbsp olive oil

### Preparation

- Peel and cut carrots into 1-inch pieces and cook in just enough water to cover.
- Withdraw from heat when half-cooked.
- Drain the carrots, place in a bowl and add garlic, well-drained caraway seeds, chili pepper, salt and oil.
- Reduce to a chunky puree, which should stay thick enough to be spreadable. Eat cold.

# Celery Seeds
## in the Kitchen

The slightly bitter taste of celery seeds perfumes home made stocks, soups, pot roasts and stews, and adds a little something to curries and Indian *garam masala*. Dry sautéing the seeds before grinding enhances their flavor.

### Buying and Storing
Ground celery seeds go rancid quickly. It's better to frequently prepare small batches of ground celery.

# Baked Eggs with Celery Seeds

These nutritious and fun little ramekins allow us to benefit from all the virtues of celery and make a delicious vegetarian appetizer.

### Ingredients for 4
1 celery stalk

4 tbsp 15% cooking cream

1 tbsp 35% cooking cream

½ tsp celery seeds

4 very fresh eggs

### Preparation
- Preheat the oven to 350°F (180°C ).
- Wash the celery stalk, chop it very finely and add the cream and celery seeds.
- Split the mix between four ramekins and break an egg into each.
- Place the ramekins in an oven-safe dish, and pour water halfway up the edges of the.
- Put in the oven and cook for 5 minutes.
- Serve the eggs with crispy breadsticks or crostini, which your guests can dip into their potted eggs.

# Chervil
# in the Kitchen

Chervil flavors chunky soups, vinaigrettes, sauces and salads, and adds a licorice taste to omelettes and fish dishes.

## Buying and Storing

Fragile chervil can be kept in the refrigerator days in a plastic container or wrapped in a slightly damp paper towel for up to a few days.

. . . . . . . . . . . . . . . . . . . . . . . . . . . . . . . . .

**Caution**
Chervil can be toxic in large quantities.

## Asparagus with Chervil Cream

Chervil marries well with green vegetables, especially with asparagus in cream.

### Ingredients for 4

1 lb fresh asparagus

⅓ cup butter or non-hydrogenated margarine

5 tbsp chervil, chopped

1 lemon, juice and zest

Salt and pepper to taste

½ cup (125 ml) 15% cooking cream

### Preparation

- Wash asparagus and peel the stalks.
- Cover with water, bring to a boil and cook for 8 to 10 minutes depending on their thickness.
- Drain the asparagus and reserve 1 cup (250 ml) of the cooking water.
- Reduce the cooking water by half, then add butter, chopped chervil, and lemon juice and zest.
- Season with salt and pepper, then bring to a boil.
- Incorporate the cream, adjust the seasoning, and pour over the asparagus.

# Chives
## in the Kitchen

Chives bring their refined taste to thick soups, omelettes, salads, vinaigrettes and marinades, as well as to gratins, fish, seafood and quiches.

### Buying and Storing

Chives are mostly consumed fresh, but they can also be frozen. Dried chives lose the true essence of their flavor. Fresh stalks can be kept for a few days in water or in a plastic bag in the refrigerator.

## Shrimp and Chive Sauté

A simply delightful way to serve chives fresh from the garden.

### Ingredients for 4

1 clove garlic, minced

1 bunch chives, washed, dried and snipped with scissors

2 tbsp olive oil

1 lb raw large shrimp, shelled and deveined

1 dash light tamari soy sauce

2 tbsp sesame seeds

Salt and pepper

### Preparation

- Combine the chives, garlic and olive oil.
- Pour into a very hot non-stick pan or a wok, add shrimp, and quickly sauté.
- Cook for 2 minutes, stirring constantly.
- Salt and pepper to taste, then add a dash of soy sauce.
- Serve the shrimp on a green salad, sprinkled with sesame seeds and accompanied by rice and mixed vegetables.

# Cloves
## in the Kitchen

Cloves can be found in several spice blends (curry, Chinese five-spice, Arabian *ras-al-hanout*), North American cooks most often use it to flavor stocks, marinades, stews, conserves, vinegars, deli meats, and even some desserts.

### Buying and Storing
Keep cloves in a cool, dark place. The spice is ground as needed in order to retain its fragrance.

. . . . . . . . . . . . . . . . . . . . . . . . . . . . . .

### Caution
Pregnant women should use essential oils with a great deal of care and caution.

## Spiced Tea

A drink to savor slowly on a cold, snowy winter's night.

### Ingredients for 1 cup
1 pinch of Ceylon tea

2 cloves

1 cinammon stick

3 cardamom pods

1 cup (250 ml) water

Sugar to taste

### Preparation
- Boil all the ingredients for 5 minutes.
- Strain before serving and add sugar to taste.

## Aromatic Apple Compote

Less sweet than jams, compotes make the perfect light breakfast spread and are wonderful as a dessert or spooned on top of yogurt.

### Ingredients for 4
2 ¼ lbs apples (Golden or Cortland)

½ cup (125 ml) apple cider or apple juice

⅓ cup (80 ml) sugar

1 cinnamon stick

2 cloves

3 tbsp butter or non-hydrogenated margarine

Juice and zest of ½ lemon

3 tbsp water

1 tsp vanilla extract

### Preparation
- Peel apples and cut into thin slices. Cook in the cider and two-thirds of the sugar for 3 minutes over low heat.
- Add cinnamon, cloves, vanilla and the butter in pieces,. Mix and cook for about 15 minutes over medium heat. Watch it closely prevent the mixture from sticking to the bottom of the pot.
- Cook the lemon zest and juice in 3 tbsp water along with the remining sugar and pour into the compote.
- Cook until thick, about 5 to 10 minutes.
- Let cool at room temperature.

# Coriander in the Kitchen

Coriander leaves and seeds are used abundantly in traditional Middle Eastern and Asian cuisines, while the leaves alone are an extremely common ingredient in Mexican dishes.

## Buying and Storing

Dried coriander leaves, yellowish, lightly ribbed and about the size of a peppercorn, are available whole or powdered in bottles on the shelves of many fine grocers. Fresh coriander, also known as cilantro, is sold in bunches in fruit markets, grocery stores, and supermarkets. Avoid yellow-tinged leaves.

Cilantro keeps for two to three weeks in a small glass of water to keep the stalks moist. Cover the glass with a plastic bag and seal with an elastic. They can also be kept in a plastic bag or wrapped in a paper towel in the refrigerator's vegetable drawer. Separate into smaller bunches and loosely wrap in damp paper towels and then in a plastic bag. Fresh leaves can be frozen, snipped with scissors into an ice cube tray and then covered with water, or even frozen in a sealed container or plastic bag.

### Caution

Coriander or cilantro leaves (fresh or dried) are very rich in vitamin K, which the body needs to form blood clots. People who take anticoagulant medicines should carefully watch their daily intake of vitamin K, and because coriander is so high in vitamin K, it should be used as a seasoning only and not as a side dish or meal (such as, for example, a salad with a cilantro leaf base).

## Carrot Coriander Soup

In addition to combining both coriander leaves and seeds, this savory soup brings together ginger and turmeric, reknowned for their anticancer properties.

### Ingredients for 4

2 tbsp olive oil

4 medium carrots, peeled and chopped

2 medium zucchini, peeled and chopped

1 small clove garlic, minced

1 tbsp fresh ginger, minced

1 tsp turmeric

¼ tsp ground black pepper

½ tsp ground coriander

3 cups (750 ml) chicken stock

Salt and pepper to taste

2 tbsp fresh cilantro leavees, minced (for garnish)

### Preparation

- In a saucepan, heat oil and sauté carrots and zucchini. After about 2 or 3 minutes, add the garlic, ginger, turmeric and ground coriander, and mix well.

- Moisten with the stock, season with salt and pepper, and cover. Bring to a boil and then reduce the heat and leave to simmer, covered, for about 20 minutes.

- Season to taste, blend with a hand mixer and reheat.

- Garnish with cilantro leaves and serve.

# White Cumin in the Kitchen

Mostly used in the Maghreb, white cumin is added to couscous, tagines, shish kebabs and merguez sausages. It is an ingredient in many Indian curries, Sinhalese colombos and Arabian *ras-el-hanout*.

## Buying and Storing

White cumin can be used in seed form or ground, but the whole seeds keep their flavor better when stored. They will keep for up to three years in a cool, dark place. Just grind with a mortar or coffee grinder before using.

## Creamy Hummus

Whip up this tasty chickpea-based to serve as an appetizer with toasted pita triangles or as a dip for raw vegetables. The addition of yogurt makes it extra-rich and creamy.

### Ingredients

16 oz can of chickpeas, drained and rinsed

2 tbsp olive oil

1 squeeze of lemon juice

2 garlic cloves, minced

1 tsp white cumin, ground

1 tsp paprika

4 tbsp tahini (sesame paste)

¾ cup (180 ml) plain yogurt

Salt and pepper to taste

### Preparation

- In a food processor, combine the chickpeas, oil, lemon juice, garlic, cumin, paprika, salt, pepper and tahini.
- Blend until smooth.
- Add yogurt, taste, adjust the seasoning as desired and mix again.
- Cover with plastic wrap and refrigerate until ready to serve.

# Black Cumin in the Kitchen

Highly valued in Asian cuisine, black cumin, also called nigella, is used in making *naan* bread as well as many salads and grain, potato, fish, and rice dishes.

## Buying and Storing

Black cumin from Egypt, cultivated in large oases in the Arabian desert, is generally considered to be the best. The seeds are matte, black and very aromatic. Cumin can be bought as a powder, but it preserves its characteristics better when kept whole. It keeps for up to three years when stored in a cool, dark place. Just grind as needed with a mortar and pestle or a coffee grinder.

## Black Cumin Quinoa Cakes

The beneficial properties of cumin are combined here with nutritious quinoa, which contains all the essential amino acids needed for the body to stay healthy.

### Ingredients for 4

1 cob of corn, cooked *al dente*

$2/3$ cup (150 ml) quinoa, carefully rinsed several times

1 ¼ cups (310 ml) water

2 eggs, beaten

1 tsp pureed garlic

1 tbsp ground black cumin

Salt and pepper to taste

### Preparation

- Preheat the oven to 400°F (200°C).
- In a pot, bring quinoa and water to a boil. Cook, uncovered, for 20 minutes or until the water is entirely absorbed.
- In a bowl, combine the corn, quinoa, beaten eggs, garlic, and cumin, and then season with salt and pepper.
- Place a sheet of parchment paper on a baking sheet. Using a spoon, make small patties with the quinoa mixture and place on the parchment paper.
- Cook for 15 minutes or until the patties are golden brown.

# Turmeric
## in the Kitchen

Turmeric is the main ingredient in Indian curries and *garam masala*, and is widely used in Indian and Asian cuisines. Over the last few years, thanks to its remarkable therapeutic properties, it has become a popular addition to different cuisines across the globe, and is used in the preparation of all kinds of dishes, from soups to desserts.

### Buying and Storing

Purchase powdered turmeric in small quantities because its taste fades quickly. The powder should be kept in a sealed container, in a cool, dry, dark place. It's possible to find fresh turmeric in some Asian grocery stores; it will keep for one or two weeks in the refrigerator in a perforated plastic bag.

### Caution

If taking anticoagulants and antiplatelets or in the case of gastroduodenal ulcers or bile stones, it is not recommended to exceed 300 mg of curcumin (about 1 tbsp of turmeric) over a period of two days. Avoid consuming during pregnancy, as it was traditionally used to treat amenorrhea (the absence of menstrual blood). Pregnant women should avoid ingesting turmeric powder and extract.

## Turmeric Avocado Spread

Combining the protective benefits of avocado, tomato and pepper, this spread perfumed with turmeric also makes an excellent dip.

### Ingredients for 4

2 very ripe avocados

Juice of ½ lemon

2 tbsp red onion, finely chopped

1 ripe tomato, finely diced

½ red pepper, diced

Chili peppers to taste

1 tsp garlic, minced

2 tbsp sesame seeds

1 tsp ground turmeric

¼ tsp pepper

Salt to taste

### Preparation

- Mash the avocados with a fork and add lemon juice and diced vegetables..
- Sprinkle with sesame seeds, add the turmeric and pepper, and mix well.
- Taste and adjust the seasoning to taste.
- Serve spread on bread or as a dip with raw vegetables.

# Tandoori Fish

The famous tandoori yogurt and spice sauce gets its name from the *tandoor*, an oven used in Indian cuisine. This exotic marinade tenderizes the fish while giving it a deliciously warm aroma.

## Ingredients for 4

4 fish fillets, about ¼ lb each

2 garlic cloves, minced

½ cup (125 ml) plain yogurt

1 tsp curry powder

1 tsp turmeric

¼ tsp black pepper

1 tsp honey (or maple syrup)

1 tbsp canola oil

Salt and pepper to taste

## Preparation

- Preheat the oven to 425°F (220°C).
- In a dish large enough to fit all the fillets, combine garlic, yogurt, spices, honey and oil.
- Season the fish fillets with salt and pepper and coat with marinade. Marinate for 2 hours in the fridge.
- Wrap fish fillets in squares of parchment paper. Place on a baking sheet and put in the oven.
- Cook for 12 to 15 minutes.

# Turmeric
# in the Kitchen

## *Lentil Soup*

This spicy soup is made with so many deliciously healthy ingredients that it doesn't even need stock.

### Ingredients for 4

1 tbsp olive oil

1 onion, chopped

1 medium carrot, diced

1 celery stick, diceds

3 garlic cloves, minced

½ tsp coriander seeds, ground

½ tsp cumin seeds, ground

1 tsp turmeric

¼ tsp ground black pepper

A few pinches cardamom

½ cup (125 ml) dried red lentils, rinsed

2 tbsp tomato paste

4 cups (1/4 gallon) stock or water

A few drops chili sauce

Sel et poivre au goût

### Preparation

- In a saucepan, heat the oil over medium heat and soften the onion, diced carrot and celery.
- Add the garlic and spices and cook for 2 minutes.
- Add the lentils and tomato paste, pour in stock or water, and cover. Bring to a boil, reduce heat, and let simmer for 20 to 30 minutes.
- Season with salt and pepper, taste, adjust seasoning, add a bit of chili sauce to taste, and serve.

# Curry Leaves
## in the Kitchen

### Buying and Storing
Curry leaves can be found in most quality Indian grocery stores. Measure about 1 tbsp for a dish serving 4 to 6 people.

## *Pork and Potato Curry*

In this recipe, dried spices are toasted before being ground and added to the meat—the real secret to making a great curry.

### Ingredients for 4
½ tsp cumin seeds

½ tsp fennel seeds

½ tsp black mustard seeds

½ tsp fenugreek seeds

½ tsp coriander seeds

½ tsp black pepper

1 tsp turmeric powder

7 curry leaves

1 tbsp olive oil

2-inch piece ginger, chopped

1 medium onion, chopped

4 garlic cloves, minced

1 ½ lb cubed stewing pork

1 cup (250 ml) water

4 potatoes, quartered

1 cup (250 ml) light coconut milk

### Preparation
- In a small non-stick pan, lightly toast the cumin, fennel, black mustard, fenugreek and coriander seeds with the black peppercorns and curry leaves. Let cool and grind in a spice grinder.
- In a large non-stick pan, heat the oil and add the ginger, onion and garlic, and cook for 2 minutes.
- Add the cubed pork, spices and water, and cook, stirring, for 5 minutes over vigorous heat.
- Cover, reduce heat to low, and let simmer for 40 minutes.
- Add potatoes and cook, covered, for another 20 min.
- Add coconut milk, stir well, and let simmer for 5 more minutes.
- Serve on a bed of basmati rice.

## Superfood Smoothie

This recipe unites the best cancer-fighting and cancer-preventing foods. Drink a glass every morning.

### Ingredients

2 cups unsweetened organic soy milk

½ cup plain yogurt, preferably probiotic

30 firm red or black grapes

½ ripe avocado (the flesh should give slightly when pressed with a finger)

½ cup frozen cranberries

½ cup frozen blueberries

3 or 4 fresh or frozen strawberries

¾-inch piece ginger, peeled

1 tsp licorice powder (optional)

¼ tsp ground cinammon

2 heaping tsp turmeric

¼ tsp black pepper, finely ground

Honey, sugar or sugar substitute to taste

### Preparation

- In a food processor, combine all the ingredients and blend at maximum speed until smooth.

# Superfood Soup

The ingredients in this tangy soup have the best reputation for fighting and preventing cancer.

## Ingredients for 8 cups

3 tbsp olive oil

1 onion, quartered

1-inch piece of ginger, finely chopped

4 tsp turmeric

½ tsp freshly ground black pepper

12 Brussels sprouts

28 oz can Italian tomatoes

3 carrots, julienned

4 cups water or homemade chicken stock

2 tsp mixed herbs (basil, oregano, savory, thyme, mint)

1 tsp honey

## Preparation

- In a large saucepan, heat the oil and sauté the onion.
- Add all the other ingredients, cover, and bring to a boil.
- Reduce heat and let simmer for 20 minutes.
- Let cool and puree with a blender.

# Tarragon
## in the Kitchen

Tarragon pairs beautifully with poultry and rabbit, but salmon and scallop lovers are also fans of its delicate flavor. That said, it goes well with almost all mayonnaises, sauces, and marinades.

### Buying and Storing
Dried tarragon keeps well when stored in a dark, dry place in a sealed container. Fresh tarragon can also be preserved in vinegar.

### Caution
Tarragon essential oil is very strong and shouldn't be given to children under six.

## Tarragon Vinegar

Nothing is easier than making your own flavored vinegar! Here's a basic recipe that will kick-start your creativity and get you making vinegar with your other favorite herbs.

### Ingredients
5 sprigs tarragon, cleaned and dried

2 cups (500 ml) white or red vinegar with 5% acetic acid

### Preparation
- Place torn herbs into a bottle. Cover with vinegar and seal.
- Refrigerate for 1 month.
- Strain using a coffee filter transfer liquid to a clean bottle.
- Store vinegar away from light.

## Green Vegetable and Tarragon Soup

A great friend to green vegetables and potatoes, tarragon gives this smooth soup its lovely subtle anise flavor.

### Ingredients for 6
4 large potatoes, peeled and chopped

1 broccoli, washed and separated into florets

1 cup green beans, chopped

1 clove garlic, minced

1 onion, chopped

1 tbsp canola oil

2 tbsp 15% cooking cream

2 tbsp tarragon, chopped

4 cups vegetable or chicken stock

Salt and pepper to taste

### Preparation
- In a pot, heat oil and sauté the onion.
- Add vegetables, minced garlic and tarragon.
- Pour in the stock, cover, and bring to a boil.
- Reduce heat and cook at a low boil for 20 minutes or just until all the vegetables are fully cooked.
- Puree with a blender or a hand blender and season with salt and pepper to taste.
- Return to the stove, reheat, and add the cream at the last minute.

# Fenugreek
## in the Kitchen

Fenugreek is chiefly used in Egyptian and Ethiopian cuisine, but vegetarians and raw food aficionados have had fenugreek on the menu for years because of the spice's quick sprouting, and its popularity is slowly but surely growing in North America and Europe.

### Buying and Storing

Fenugreek seeds are used dried, whole, ground, crushed or as sprouts, untoasted and toasted, but they are most fragrant when they are toasted and ground. Store them in a sealed container in a cool, dark, and dry place. Fenugreek oil is reknowned for its softening effect on the skin and its anti-inflammatory properties.

### Caution

Because it stimulates the uterus, fenugreek is not recommended during pregnancy.

## Spiced Lamb

Here is another recipe that uses the dry toasting method, which brings out the spices' fragrance.

### Ingredients for 4

½ tsp fenugreek seeds

½ tsp caraway seeds

½ tsp cumin seeds

½ tsp peppercorns

½ tsp coriander seeds

½ tsp cardamom seeds

1 tsp Indian curry powder

1 tsp ginger powder

2 large onions, finely chopped

2 cloves garlic, minced

4 lamb chops or 1 ½ lbs cubed lamb

28 oz can of tomatoes, crushed with a hand blender

14 oz can of coconut milk

2 tbsp olive oil

Fresh cilantro leaves

### Preparation

- Lightly toast the dry spices in a hot pan, then crush them with a mortar and pestle or in a coffee grinder. Add the curry powder and ginger.

- In an oven-safe pot, soften the onions and garlic in a bit of oil.

- Remove and set aside.

- In the saucepan, brown the lamb for a few minutes in oil, then add the softened onions and garlic.

- Add the chopped tomatoes to the meat along with the coconut milk and spices.

- Cook for about 20 minutes over medium heat, uncovered, so that the cooking juices reduce.

- Serve with basmati rice and garnish with cilantro.

- For a spicier dish, add hot peppers or curry paste.

# Juniper Berries
## in the Kitchen

Juniper berries are in great demand during game season because they are perfect for seasoning wild meat stews, roasts, and stocks, and in tasty tenderizing marinades.

### Buying and Storing

Store berries in a sealed container in a cool, dark, dry place. To get even more flavor out of them, crush right before adding to a dish.

### Caution

Because it stimulates the uterus, juniper berries are not recommended during pregnancy. In fact, they were traditionally used to induce delivery.

## Quail with Juniper Berries

Stuffed with prosciutto and mushrooms, these quail make a succulent appetizer before a pasta or salad main course.

### Ingredients for 4 (as an appetizer)

4 quails, trussed

1 tbsp olive oil

¼ cup (60 ml) prosciutto, chopped

6 mushrooms, chopped

1 dried shallot, minced

3 garlic cloves, minced

½ tsp dried herbs (oregano and basil) or fresh (rosemary and savory)

Salt and pepper to taste

20 juniper berries

1 tbsp olive oil

1 tbsp flour

1 tbsp orange marmalade

¼ cup (60 ml) white wine

½ cup (60 ml) stock

⅓ cup (80 ml) 15% cream

### Preparation

- In a pan, sauté dried shallot in oil for 3 minutes.
- Add the chopped prosciutto, mushrooms, garlic and herbs, and cook for another 3 minutes. Season with salt and pepper and add juniper berries.
- Stuff the quails with this mixture and close the openings with skewers.
- Heat 1 tbsp olive oil in a pan and brown quails on each side. Remove and set aside.
- In the same pan, combine the flour, marmalade, white wine and stock and bring to a boil. Return the quails to the pan, cover, and cook 15 min.
- Uncover, add the cream and stir, cook 3 min and serve.

# Ginger
## in the Kitchen

Ginger's spicy bite and unique freshness make it one of the most versatile foods there is. It adds kick to soups, fish and poultry as well as to salads and desserts. Ginger is a longtime favorite of Asian cuisine, and in North America both the fresh and dried spice are quickly becoming refrigerator and pantry staples.

### Buying and Storing

Ginger is sold fresh, dried or pickled and can also be ground or candied. Young ginger root is very fragrant and juicy. Look for a bulb that is firm, mold-free and not withered. Fresh ginger keeps in the refrigerateur for two to three weeks, but store it on a shelf instead of in the vegetable drawer, which is too humid and may cause it to rot more quickly. It can also be kept fresh in the pantry, like onions and potatoes, but do not peel it until ready to use. Freeze the root whole in a freezer bag and simply cut off pieces as needed and grate while the ginger is still frozen, as thawed ginger is more difficult to grate. Make marinated ginger by placing the unpeeled roots in a jar of brandy or sherry. It will keep indefinitely if it is stored, tightly sealed, in the refrigerator.

Store ground ginger in a sealed container and keep in a cool, dark, dry place. Powdered or ground ginger goes stale quickly and is easily contaminated.

Candied ginger will keep indefinitely. Pickled ginger should be refrigerated after opening.

## Ginger Orange Salmon

Is there a better duo than ginger and fish? Here's a simple recipe that lets us truly appreciate this simple pairing.

### Ingredients for 2

1 tbsp canola oil

4 green onions, chopped

1 tsp sesame oil

1 tbsp tamari soy sauce

1 tbsp fresh ginger, minced

1 tsp honey

2 tbsp orange juice (or clementine juice)

2 salmon fillets

Pepper to taste

### Preparation

- Place the canola oil and green onions on a microwave-safe plate and microwave on high for 1 minute.

- On the same plate, combine cooked onions with the sesame oil, tamari sauce, ginger, honey and orange juice. Coat fish with the mixture and cover with wax paper or plastic wrap without tightening or sealing it.

- Cook for 2 minutes on medium-high heat.

- Flip the fillets and cook for 1 minute more.

- Test for doneness and continue cooking on medium-high if necessary.

- Remove from the microwave, season with pepper and taste, and let rest for 3 minutes. Strain sauce, ladle over fish, and serve.

# Ginger
# in the Kitchen

## Shrimp, Scallop and Ginger Pasta

Here is a yummy way to benefit from the powerful antioxidant and anti-aging properties of ginger, turmeric and pepper.

### Ingredients for 2

6 oz short pasta

3 tbsp canola or grapeseed oil

3 green onions, thinly sliced

5 slices ginger, peeled and minced

1 clove garlic, minced

½ tsp curry powder

½ tsp turmeric

¼ tsp pepper

2 tbsp unbleached flour

¾ cup tomatoes, crushed with a hand blender

½ cup 15% cooking cream

8 large shrimp

10 medium scallops

3 tbsp cilantro leaves

Salt and pepper to taste

### Preparation

- In a large pot of salted boiling water, cook the pasta *al dente* according to the package directions.
- In the meantime, heat a skillet over high heat for 2 minutes, pour in oil, and sauté the green onion, ginger and garlic for 2 minutes.
- Add the curry powder, turmeric, pepper and flour, and cook for 1 minute, stirring constantly with a wooden spoon.
- Add tomaotes, still stirring constantly, and then pour in the cream and bring to a boil.
- Poach the scallops and shrimp in the boiling sauce, reduce the temperature slightly, and cook for 2 to 3 minutes.
- Taste and adjust the seasoning if desired.
- Drain the cooked pasta and toss to coat with seafood sauce.
- Garnish with fresh cilantro leaves and serve.

## Rice with Ginger and Peppers

Peppers, celery seeds, chili sauce and ginger are all packed with antioxidants and will help ease joint pain with their anti-inflammatory properties.

### Ingredients for 4

2 tbsp olive oil

White base of 1 leek, thinly sliced, or 2 dried shallots, very thinly sliced

½ red pepper, diced

½ yellow pepper, diced

½ tsp celery seeds, ground

½ tsp chili sauce

1-inch piece ginger, grated

1 cup long-grain rice

2 cups of water, salted to taste

### Preparation

- In a large microwavable bowl 8-cup measuring cup, combine the oil, leek or shallots and the diced pepper. Heat for 1 minute on high.
- Add the rice, celery seeds, chili sauce and ginger, mix well and cook again for 1 minute on high.
- Add the salted water and cook for 8 minutes on high
- Continue cooking for 10 minutes on medium.
- Let rest for 5 minutes before serving.

# Bay Leaves
## in the Kitchen

The bay leaf is more known for its fragrance than its taste, and is a common ingredient in soups, stews and dishes with savory sauces. Slip a few leaves into a small jar of oil and drizzle the slightly floral seasoning over salads or dips.

### Buying and Storing

The bay laurel tree is known for its dark green and glossy leaves and small yellow flowers. The leaves are sold dried and will keep for a long time if stored in a dark, dry place, and impart a much stronger aroma when torn or broken.

### Caution

Choose bay leaves with caution, as some members of the laurel family are poisonous.

# Ratatouille Provençale

## Ingredients for 4

3 tbsp olive oil

1 onion, sliced

1 yellow pepper, seeds and membranes removed, julienned

1 orange pepper, seeds and membranes removed, julienned

1 zucchini, cut into rounds

½ fennel bulb, thinly sliced

3 garlic cloves, minced

1 eggplant, sliced

28 oz can of tomatoes, mixed with a hand blender

½ cup white wine

1 bunch fresh herbs (thyme, oregano, rosemary) or 1 tsp *herbes de Provence*

4 bay leaves

Salt and pepper to taste

## Preparation

- Preheat oven to 300°F (150°C).

- Heat a large frying pan, add 1 tbsp olive oil and and sauté the onion and peppers for 3 minutes. Transfer to a large casserole dish with a cover and place in the oven.

- In the same frying pan, add another 1 tbsp oil and sauté the zucchini, fennel and garlic for about 2 minutes. Spoon over the onions and peppers.

- Add the rest of the oil to the pan and sauté the eggplant slices for 2 minutes.

- Layer over the vegetables in the casserole dish.

- In the frying pan, combine the tomatoes, white wine, herbs, bay leaves and seasonings, and bring to a boil. Pour the mixutre into the dish and return to the oven.

- Cook for 1 hour or until vegetables are cooked.

- Serve as an appetizer or alongside grilled meat or fish.

# Peppermint in the Kitchen

Peppermint is a much-loved herb in Greece and the Middle East, where it is used liberally in raw and cooked dishes. It is also used to make famously tasty infusions, syrups and luscious desserts. In North America, it is often combined with leg of lamb, fruit salads and dark chocolate.

## Buying and Storing

Mint leaves must be fresh and green, free of stains and yellowing. They will keep from a few days to a week in the refrigerator if the stalks wrapped in a damp paper towel and then a plastic bag. To freeze mint leaves, chop and place them in an ice cube tray, fill the tray with fresh water, and freeze for several hours. Dry mint by removing the leaves from their stalks and spreading them onto a nylon mosquito net. To preserve their flavor, only grind the leaves into a powder when they are ready to use and store in a sealed container in a cool, dry place. Chopped mint can also be soaked in oil or vinegar. Leave to soak for one or two weeks, then strain and use.

## Caution

The plant is not recommended for children under six due to the risk of laryngeal spasms (contraction of the larynx), or for pregnant or breastfeeding women.

## *Tzatziki*

### Ingredients

1 cucumber

7 or 8 fresh mint leaves

2 garlic cloves, crushed

1 cup (250 ml) plain yogurt (Greek or Bulgarian)

1 tbsp olive oil

Salt and pepper to taste

### Preparation

- Peel and seed the cucumber, then grate it and drain it for at least 15 minutes to remove as much juice as possible.
- Chop the mint leaves and combine with the garlic.
- Mix together the yogurt, olive oil, chopped mint, garlic, cucumber, salt and pepper, and chill in the refrigerator for at least 1 hour.
- Serve with toasted bread or as a sauce for meat, such as grilled lamb.
- For a zingy variation, add dill, lemon zest and juice or some finely chopped green onions.

# Mustard
# in the Kitchen

Mustard seeds are an important ingredient in most flavorful rubs, and they sprout into a nutritious green that adds a hot bite to salads. Prepared mustards are wonderful in mayonnaises and vinaigrettes and add zip to sauces and meats.

## Buying and Storing

Prepared mustard is stored in the refrigerator in a sealed container; it loses its flavor at room temperature. Mustard powders and whole seeds are stored in a cool, dry, dark place. Fragile mustard leaves can be stored, unwashed, for a few days in a perforated plastic bag in the refrigerator and can be frozen like spinach. Mustard oil should be stored the refrigerator or somewhere cool.

Prepared mustard is a combination of ground, whole, cracked or bruised mustard seeds, vinegar, water and salt. Mustard connoisseurs claim that the darker the mustard, the higher the quality.

## Rabbit with Two-Mustard Sauce

Rabbit with mustard sauce is a classic French dish, and when cream is added, this succulent meat will please even the pickiest palates.

### Ingredients for 4

2 tbsp olive oil

1 rabbit (about 3 lb), cut into pieces

2 tbsp Dijon mustard

2 tbsp whole grain mustard

1 small onion, whole

1 garlic clove, whole

1 bay leaf

1 tsp tarragon

Salt and pepper to taste

¾ cup (180 ml) white wine

¾ cup (180 ml) chicken stock

¼ cup (60 ml) 15% cooking cream

1 tbsp cornstarch thinned with a bit of water

### Preparation

- Preheat the oven to 350°F (180°C).
- Combine the two mustards and brush onto the rabbit.
- In an oven-safe pan, heat oil and brown the rabbit on all sides.
- Add the onion, garlic, bay leaf, tarragon, salt and pepper. Add the white wine and stock, then heat until it comes to a boil.
- Cover the pan  and place in the oven.
- Cook for 1 hour or until rabbit is very tender.
- To make the sauce, remove the meat and keep warm. Discard the onion, garlic and bay leaf, reheat the cooking juices, and add the cream and the watered-down cornstarch, stirring constantly until it thickens.
- Serve with pasta and green beans.

# Nutmeg
## in the Kitchen

This piquant brown spice warms up potages, gratins, purees, vegetables, quiches and soufflés.

### Buying and Storing
A good quality nutmeg seed will release a small amount of oil when squeezed. Whole nutmeg should be stored in a dry place and should keep for three or four years. Ground nutmeg should be stored in a jar in a dry, dark place.

### Caution
The fragrant nutmeg seed contains myristicin, harmful to the nervous system if taken in very large doses.

# *Cauliflower Gratin*

Nutmeg really highlights the cheesy creaminess of this classic comfort food, perfect as an appetizer or alongside grilled meat or fish.

### Ingredients for 4
1 large cauliflower, trimmed and separated into florets

3 tbsp butter or non-hydrogenated margarine

3 tbsp flour

1 ½ cups (375 ml) milk

1 cup (250 ml) grated cheese (Gruyère or emmental)

½ tsp nutmeg

Salt and pepper to taste

### Preparation
- In a large pot, cook cauliflower in salted boiling water for 15 minutes and drain.
- To make the sauce, first melt the butter in a pot over low heat.
- Add the sifted flour and mix until fully incorporated.
- Add the milk and stir constantly until the sauce thickens.
- Season with salt and pepper. Grate nutmeg into the béchamel sauce. Remove from heat and add half of the grated cheese.
- Mix just until the fromage is melted into the sauce.
- Place the cooked cauliflower into a casserole dish.
- Pour the béchamel over the cauliflower.
- Sprinkle with the remaining grated cheese.
- Broil for 5 minutes until golden brown.

# Oregano
## in the Kitchen

Oregano is one of the favorite herbs of Italian cuisine. It is the constant companion of tomatoes and absolutely indispensable to pizzas and sauces. Because it is known to prevent gas and bloating, oregano is also frequently added to bean and legume dishes.

### Buying and Storing

Dried oregano is available year-round in grocery stores, or can be bought fresh in the summer. Look for brightly-colored leaves with a strong odor, and avoid leaves that are brown or wilted. Wrap the leaves loosely in a slightly damp paper towel and keep in the refrigerator for up to three days. To dry fresh oregano, spread the sprigs on a rack in a dark, well-ventilated area for three to five days or until they become crisp. They can also be spread out on a paper towel and cooked in the microwave for 2 minutes on high. Throw out any blackened leaves.

To freeze it, finely chop fresh oregano and place it in ice cube trays with a bit of water. To serve, simply mix an oregano ice cube into cooked food as needed.

Dried oregano is sold as chopped or ground leaves. Store the dried herbs in a sealed container in a dark, well-ventilated area.

### Caution

Used externally, the essential oil of oregano should be used with caution because it will irritate the skin and can even be corrosive. Used internally, never exceed the recommended dose because it may irritate the digestive tract.

# Tomato Oregano Pizza

The simplicity of this classic pizza lets you truly savor each delicious individual ingredient.

### Ingredients

1 package store-bought pizza dough

1 cup (250 ml) homemade tomato sauce

1 clove garlic, chopped

½ tsp dried oregano

Salt and pepper

1 lb mozzarella cheese

6 anchovy fillets

### Preparation

- Preheat the oven to 450°F (230°C).
- Roll out the pizza dough on an oiled pan or a pizza stone and fold the edges over to make a crust.
- Spread the sauce evenly over the dough, sprinkle with minced garlic and oregano, and season with salt and pepper.
- Thinly slice the mozzarella cheese and distribute evenly over the sauce. Layer the anchovies on top of the cheese.
- Cook for 20 minutes in the oven.

# Paprika
## in the Kitchen

Paprika flavors soups, sauces and vinaigrettes and long-simmering dishes like goulash, a Hungarian beef stew, would not be the same without it.

### Buying and Storing
It is better to store paprika in the refrigerator because its color and flavor deteriorate quickly. Store away from light and heat, preferably in the freezer.

### Chef's Secret
Whip up a batch of appetizing health-smart oven-baked French fries seasoned with paprika, and add color to dips and cold sauces like hummus (p. 136), cooked sauces, and mayonnaises.

## *Hungarian Goulash*

### Ingredients
2 lb well-marbled stewing beef, cubed

1 heaping tbsp unbleached flower

2 tbsp olive oil

2 onions, finely chopped

2 garlic cloves, minced

½ tsp savory

1 tsp caraway seeds

1 cup chicken stock

1 tbsp paprika

Salt and pepper to taste

¾ cup (180 ml) sour cream

### Preparation
- Preheat the oven to 300°F (150°C).
- Coat beef cubes with flour.
- In an oven-safe pan, heat 1 tbsp olive oil and sauté the onions for 3 minutes. Remove and set aside.
- Pour the remaining oil into the pan and brown the beef cubes on each side. Add garlic, savory, caraway seeds, and enough stock to cover the meat. Return the onions to the pan, cover, and bring to a boil.
- Cook in the oven for 1 hour.
- After 1 hour, remove from the oven, add paprika, and season with salt and pepper. Return to the oven and cook for another 30 minutes.
- Shortly before serving, add a dollop of pan sauce to the sour cream and mix well.
- Pour sour cream mixture into the pot and heat gently without letting it boil.
- Serve with pasta and steamed vegetables.

# Parsley
## in the Kitchen

Tabbouleh's main ingredient is also the world's most popular herb! Parsley is so much more than a garnish—it is a storehouse of nutrients and should be enjoyed in a host of different savory dishes.

### Buying and Storing

Look for fresh parsley with nice firm stalks and bright green leaves. Place the stalks in a glass of water while it's still fresh. Wash the leaves first because there will often be hiding a bit of dirt or sand. Swish it gently in a bowl of water, wipe dry, and store, if desired, in a perforated plastic bag in the vegetable drawer. Parsley also freezes well: simply snip the leaves with scissors into an ice cube tray and cover with water.

Parsley can be dried by hanging it upside-down in bunches in a dark, well-ventilated area, but it will lose a lot of its nutrients. It is better to buy fresh parsley, since it is inexpensive and available year-round.

### Chef's Secret

Use curly parsley's stems and leaves to add toothsome crunch in your salads and soups and to benefit from the healing properties of the entire plant.

## Taboulleh

This salad is packed with vitamin-rich parsley and mint. Try it with bulghur instead of couscous!

### Ingredients for four or more

¾ cup (180 ml) couscous

¾ cup (180 ml) boiling water

1 red onion, finely chopped

2 or 3 tomatoes, seeded and diced

1 tightly packed cup (250 ml) fresh parsley, finely chopped

¼ cup (60 ml) fresh peppermint, chopped

3 tbsp olive oil

1 tbsp lemon juice

Salt and pepper to taste

### Preparation

- In a bowl, pour boiling water over couscous. Cover and let sit for 5 minutes.
- Fluff with a fork.
- Add the onion, tomatoes, parsley and mint.
- In a small bowl, combine the oil, lemon juice, salt and pepper. Pour over salad and mix well.

. . . . . . . . . . . . . . . . . . . . . . . . . . . . .

### Note

This recipe is even better prepared in advance. Make it even healthier by adding chopped seeded cucumber or diced peppers, or even chopped Kalamata olives.

# Chili Peppers
# in the kitchen

Thousands of different varieties of chili peppers can be found in the local markets of Asia, Africa and Latin America, where they are the star of savory foods including soups, fish dishes, meat dishes, sauces, and oils . Many innovative chefs are even using chilis to spice up chocolate- and fruit-based desserts.

## Buying and Storing

Chili peppers are sold dried and fresh. Choose fresh peppers that are brightly-colored, without stains or soft spots. Fresh chilis can be stored in a paper bag in the refrigerator, but will start losing flavor after about one week. They can also be frozen, dried, ground, or made into a powder. Dried chili peppers, whole or powdered, can be stored in a sealed container in a cool, dark place for about one year. Tabasco sauce keeps indefinitely at room temperature. Harissa should be refrigerated after opening.

## Harissa

A spicy Tunisian chili sauce typically used in small amounts.

### Ingredients for ½ cup

5 small fresh chili peppers (or dried, soaked in hot water for 1 hour)

2 garlic cloves, minced

2 tsp coriander seeds

2 tsp cumin seeds

2 tsp caraway seeds

1 pinch salt

½ cup (125 ml) olive oil

### Preparation

- Wearing gloves, remove the seeds from the fresh chilis or drain and pat dry the rehydrated peppers. Place in a small food processor.
- Add the spices and mix together on high speed.
- Pour the oil into the food processor in a steady stream.
- Transfer into a small glass pot, pour in a bit of oil, and seal.
- Keeps at least 6 weeks in the refrigerator.

# Duck with Spicy Beer Sauce

Heat things up in the kitchen with this fiery, unbelievably moist duck dish that is perfect for sharing.

## Ingredients for 2

1 duck breast, divided into two portions (or 1 small breast each)

½ cup (125 ml) amber beer

3 garlic cloves, sliced

1-inch piece ginger, peeled and thinly sliced

1 tbsp orange marmalade

1 heaping tsp mixed ground seeds (mustard, fennel, cumin and coriander)

¼ tsp ground chili pepper

Salt to taste

## Preparation

- Preheat the oven to 400°F (200°C).
- Spread the spice mix in the bottom of a shallow dish. Press duck breasts, flesh side down, into the mixture to create a crust. Remove. Using a knife, cut a diamond pattern into the fat. Set aside.
- In the same dish, combine the beer, garlic, ginger, orange marmalade and ground chili pepper. Place duck in the dish, skin side up. Cover and marinate in the refrigerator for about 3 hours.
- Take the duck out of the refrigerator 30 minutes before cooking, remove from the marinade, and set aside.
- Strain marinade and set aside.
- Heat a heavy-bottomed oven-safe pan and brown the duck, skin side down, for 3 minutes. Flip and cook for another 2 minutes.
- Discard the pan juices and transfer the duck back to the pan, skin side down. Pour half of the marinade over the duck, cover with a sheet of aluminum foil, and cook in the oven for 10 minutes for medium rare or 20 minutes for well-done.
- To make the sauce, remove the duck from the pan and keep warm. Discard cooking fat.
- Deglaze the pan with the remaining marinade and reduce for 1 minute.
- Taste, season with salt as needed. Spoon sauce over duck and serve with a salad and baked potato.

# Chili Peppers
# in the Kitchen

## *Fish Pasta Medley*

Here's a reason for pasta lovers to celebrate—this piquant fish pasta is delicious and loaded with healthy goodness!

### Ingredients for 4

14 oz spaghetti

2 tbsp olive oil

1 yellow pepper, seeded and julienned

2 garlic cloves, minced

2 medium zucchinis, thinly sliced

2 cups (500 ml) canned tomatoes, chopped with a hand blender

4 anchovy fillets, rinsed and chopped

¼ cup (60 ml) black olives, minced

¼ tsp chili pepper flakes

Salt and pepper to taste

2 tbsp basil leaves

4 sole fillets, cut into bite-sized pieces

### Preparation

- In a pot of salted boiling water, cook the pasta al dente according to package instructions. Drain and set aside.

- While the pasta is cooking, heat the oil in a heavy-bottomed pan over medium heat and soften the pepper, about 4 minutes.

- Add garlic, zucchini, tomatoes, anchovy fillets, black olives and chili flakes.

- Bring to a boil, reduce heat and let simmer, uncovered, for 20 minutes.

- Taste, season with salt and pepper as needed, and add basil and fish.

- Let simmer for 5 to 7 minutes until the fish is cooked.

- Serve over the cooked pasta.

# Jamaican Allspice in the Kitchen

Because of its peppery taste, some prefer Jamaican allspice to cloves to flavor meat pies and stews, marinades, and pickles.

## Buying and Storing

Stores sell both Jamaican allspice seeds and ground allspice. However, it is better to buy the seeds and grind it yourself, small amounts at a time, to preserve the flavor. Store in a tightly sealed jar in a dry, dark place.

## Spiced Veal Burgers

Put a spin on burger night by serving warm spiced veal patties with carrot, ginger, allspice, and orange zest.

### Ingredients for 4

1 lb ground veal

1 tbsp ginger, minced

½ cup (125 ml) carrot, grated

½ cup (125 ml) rolled oats

1 small onion (or 2 dried shallots), grated

1 egg, beaten

1 tsp orange zest

¼ tsp cumin seeds

¼ tsp coriander seeds

¼ tsp Jamaican allspice

¼ tsp dried basil

¼ tsp dried mint

Salt and pepper to taste

### Preparation

- In a bowl, combine the ground veal, ginger, carrot, rolled oats, onion (or shallot), beaten egg, orange zest and spices.
- Gently mix, and season with salt and pepper.
- Cook for 10 minutes on the barbecue or in a grill pan, flipping the patties halfway through.
- Serve with potato salad (p.188) and green vegetables.

# Pepper
## in the Kitchen

Pepper is so valuable in cooking that it changed the course of history, and it would be impossible to list every dish, country, and type of cuisine that use it. These days, contemporary chefs are even adding it to dark chocolate and fruity desserts.

### Buying and Storing

Pepper loses its flavor quickly, so it is best to buy whole peppercorns and keep them in a wood pepper grinder, which allows you to choose the size of the grind and season food as needed. Look for solid, heavy, uniformly-colored peppercorns, and choose a quality brand to avoid paying for something other than pepper. Whole peppercorns can be stored for about one year in a tightly sealed container, preferably in the refrigerator; ground pepper loses its flavor after two or three months.

## Two Pepper Vegetable Soup

### Ingredients for 6 or more

2 tbsp olive oil

1 onion, diced

2 tsp ground cumin

¾ tsp ground Jamaican allspice

½ tsp cayenne pepper

½ tsp white pepper

½ tsp turmeric

1 orange pepper, diced

2 cups (500 ml) carrots, diced

2 cups (500 ml) sweet potatoes, diced

2 cups (500 ml) orange squash (butternut squash or pumpkin), diced

1 cup (250 ml) dried red lentils

1 ½ tsp salt

1 bay leaf

¼ tsp grated orange zest

½ cup (125 ml) fresh orange juice

6 cups (1/2 gallon) water

3 tbsp lemon juice

½ cup (125 ml) fresh cilantro, chopped

### Preparation

- In a large pot, heat the oil over medium-high heat and sauté the onion until translucent, about 3 minutes.

- Combine the cumin, allspice, cayenne pepper, white pepper, and turmeric, and cook for 1 minute.

- Add the pepper, carrots, sweet potatoes, squash, lentils, salt, bay leaf and orange zest and cook for 10 minutes, stirring frequently.

- Add the water and bring to a boil. Reduce the heat and let simmer until the vegetables are tender, about 30 minutes.

- Add the orange and lemon juice.

- Garnish with cilantro and serve.

# Mussels in Green Peppercorn Sauce

## Ingredients for 2

2 lbs mussels, cleaned and trimmed

½ cup (125 ml) white wine

1 bunch parsley

2 tbsp non-hydrogenated margarine

2 dried shallots, peeled and chopped

1 clove garlic, minced

2 tsp flour

8 to 10 mushrooms, quartered

1 tsp green peppercorns, pickled or in vinegar

½ tsp lemon zest

½ cup (125 ml) light coconut milk

3 tbsp fresh parsley, chopped

## Preparation

- In a large pot, combine the mussels, white wine and parsley. Cover, bring to a boil, and cook for about 3 minutes or until the mussels are open. Discard any closed mussels.

- Let cool, remove the mussels, strain the cooking juice and reserve ½ cup. Keep the remaining juice for a fish soup.

- Shell the mussels and set aside.

- In a small saucepan, melt the margarine. Sauté the shallots and garlic and then whisk in flour.

- Pour in the reserved ½ cup of cooking juices and add the mushrooms, green pepper, lemon zest, and coconut milk.

- Cook over medium heat until the sauce thickens, then transfer the mussels back to the pan.

- Serve over long pasta or on rice.

# Pepper
## in the Kitchen

## Pepper-Crusted Filet Mignon

Enjoy melt-in-your-mouth spice-encrusted filet mignon with a hint of cognac.

### Ingredients for 4

4 quality filet mignon steaks

2 tsp mixed black peppercorns, mustard seeds and caraway seeds, ground

1 tbsp olive oil

1 tbsp butter

3 tbsp cognac or whisky

2 tbsp green peppercorns preserved in vinegar

1 tsp Dijon mustard

½ cup (125 ml) 15% cooking cream

### Preparation

- Sprinkle the filet mignon steaks with the spice mixture. Store remaining spices for future use.

- Heat the oil in a skillet over medium heat, add the butter and cook the steaks for 2 minutes on each side.

- Transfer steaks to a plate and keep warm.

- Remove the pan from heat, pour in the cognac or whisky as well as the green peppercorns and mustard, bring to a boil and let boil 1 min.

- Add the cream and reduce the heat. Cook for a little longer, scraping the bottom of the pan.

- Spoon sauce over steaks and serve with a puree and green vegetables.

# Licorice
## in the Kitchen

The therapeutic benefits of licorice were not discovered until just recently, and it should definitely become a pantry staple!

### Buying and Storing

Licorice powder and sticks are available in most health food stores. It will keep for several months if stored in a cool, dark place.

### Caution

Licorice enhances the effects of some medications including digoxin, some diuretics, and corticosteroids. It's best to avoid taking them together.

## *Licorice Muffins*

Tender, moist and delicate muffins perfumed with delicately sweet licorice powder.

### Ingredients for 12 muffins

1 ½ cups (375 ml) unbleached flour

1 cup (250 ml) whole wheat flour

2/3 cup (150 ml) sugar

2 tsp baking powder

4 tsp licorice powder (in health food stores)

½ tsp salt

1 tsp cinnamon

2 eggs

1 cup (250 ml) milk

½ cup (125 ml) canola oil

### Preparation

• Preheat the oven to 375°F (180°C).

• Grease muffin tins.

• Mix the flour, sugar, baking powder, licorice powder, salt and cinnamon in a large bowl and make a hollow in the centre.

• In another bowl, beat eggs well and mix in milk and oil.

• Pour the liquid ingredients into the hollow in the dry ingredients and stir just enough to moisten.

• Transfer this mixture into the muffin tins.

• Bake in the oven on the middle rack for 17 to 20 minutes.

# Rosemary in the Kitchen

Rosemary complements a wide variety of foods including soups, marinades, grilled meats, stews, fish, seafood, vegetables, gratins and stuffings, and is even added to jams, marmalades, icings, and fruit purees.

## Buying and Storing

Fresh rosemary is at its best when it has been picked right before flowering, when it is at the peak of its flavor. It can be kept fresh on its stem for several days in a glass of water. To dry it, hang a bouquet for one or two weeks in a dark, well-ventilated area. Dried rosemary keeps for several months in a sealed container away from light. To freeze, snip the leaves with scissors into an ice cube tray and cover with water.

## Chef's Secret

To flavor grilled meats, throw a few rosemary leaves over the hot charcoal briquettes, or strip the branches of their leaves, keeping a few leaves just at the top. and use as skewers for vegetables. Cut the thin end of the stems to make threading easier.

## Greek Chicken

Wrapping the chicken breasts in parchment paper results in juicy, tender meat and seals in the savory flavor and aroma of fresh rosemary and basil.

### Ingredients for 4

4 small boneless skinless chicken breasts

2 tbsp olive oil

2 garlic cloves, minced

20 cherry tomatoes, sliced

8 black olives, pitted and chopped

8 fresh basil leaves, chopped

1 tsp fresh rosemary leaves

4 lemon slices

Salt and pepper to taste

Parchment paper and aluminum foil

### Preparation

- Preheat the oven to 400°F ( 200°C).

- Place each chicken breast on a square of lightly oiled parchment paper. Squares should be large enough to be folded into packets.

- In a bowl, combine the oil, garlic, cherry tomato slices and black olives. Spread mixture over chicken breasts.

- Season with salt and pepper and sprinkle with basil and rosemary. Top each chicken breast with a lemon slice.

- Fold the parchment paper to form four packets. Cover packets with a sheet of aluminum foil and place on a baking sheet.

- Cook in the oven for 30 minutes or until the chicken is fully cooked.

- Serve with grilled vegetables and plain rice.

# Saffron
## in the Kitchen

Saffron pairs perfectly with fish and seafood, and without it, celebrated dishes like paella and bouillabaisse would not be the same

### Buying and Storing
It's better to buy saffron threads rather than saffron powder, which is often fake. High quality saffron will tint the skin yellow, not red. The stigmas must be dark red, ¾ to 1 inch long, thin, and widened at their tips. Use 1 or 2 pistils (3 or 6 strands), depending on what you're cooking: use less for sweet dishes and more for savory dishes. Saffron must be soaked for a few minutes in hot liquid before adding to food to obtain a uniform color, but it should never be boiled.

To store saffron, place it in a sealed container and in a cool, dark, dry place. Avoid buying saffron preserved in oil or saffron with broken stigmas. The spice known as Indian saffron is actually turmeric, so pay close attention when purchasing. Mexican saffron is actually just small bunches of flavorless orange safflower petals and is commonly known as "bastard saffron." As saffron ages, it produces a spicy odor and loses its flavor and color.

Another way to preserve saffron is to infuse 10 g of pistils in 10 tablespoons of any liquid (oil, champagne, white wine, stock, cream, or milk). Let the infusion steep in the refrigerator overnight or for a few days. Use it in recipes, keeping in mind that each tablespoon of liquid equals 1/10 of a gram.

### Caution
Don't confuse the *Crocus sativus*, the plant that produces saffron, with another crocus, the colchicum, which is botanically close but highly toxic even in small doses.

## Saffron Coconut Scallops

Serve these tasty morsels as an appetizer for four or as a main dish for two.

### Ingredients for 4 (as an appetizer)
2 tbsp fortified wine (like Pineau des Charentes)

½ tsp saffron threads

1 tbsp olive oil

1 tbsp butter or non-hydrogenated margerine

1 dried shallot, minced

½ cup (125 ml) button mushrooms, wiped and thinly sliced

2 tbsp flour, levelled

¼ cup (60 ml) white wine

¾ cup (180 ml) light coconut milk

20 fresh scallops (about ¾ lb)

Pepper or Espelette pepper

2 tbsp chives, finely chopped

### Preparation
- In a small bowl, combine the saffron and the fortified wine. Let infuse at room temperature for 1 hour.
- In a hot skillet, heat the butter and oil, and sauté the shallot for 3 minutes. Add the mushrooms and sweat them just until the liquid has evaporated.
- Add the flour and mix well.
- Pour in the white wine and stir well. Add the coconut milk and allow the sauce to thicken.
- Add the scallops to the simmering sauce and poach for 3 minutes.
- Strain the fortified wine and add to the scallops and sauce.
- As an appetizer, serve the scallops in shells garnished with toasted croutons. As a main course, serve over your favourite pasta and garnish with pepper or Espelette pepper and chopped chives.

# Savory
## in the Kitchen

Savory is generally added to legume dishes, soups, sauces, and stewed meat and vegetables, but it also makes a fragrant seasoning vinegar.

### Buying and Storing

Choose a bunch of savory with bright green leaves. It is best to keep savory with its stems in a glass of water or in a perforated plastic bag in the refrigerator's vegetable bin. You can also snip its leaves with scissors and cover with water in an ice cube tray; the cubes will keep for several months in the freezer. Savory can also be dried: hang a bouquet upside-down in a dark, well-ventilated area. When the leaves become crumbly, transfer to a sealed container and store away from light.

### Caution

Savory is rich in vitamin K, which plays a role in the formation of blood clots. People taking anticoagulant medication should avoid it or consume it in very small amounts.

## Light and Fresh Potato Salad

Perfumed with savory and lemon, this is a little salad that, even without mayonnaise, proves delicious.

### Ingredients for 2

6 sprigs fresh savory, 2 whole, 4 cut with scissors

3 medium potatoes

½ tsp Dijon mustard

2 tbsp olive oil

1 small garlic clove, minced

4 tbsp plain yogurt

Zest of 1 lemon

4 green onions, finely chopped

2 tbsp fresh chives, minced

Salt and pepper to taste

### Preparation

- In a pot, boil the potatoes for 10 minutes with 2 sprigs of savory.

- In the meantime, prepare the sauce by combining the cut savory, mustard, oil and garlic in a small bowl. Mix well and let sit at room temperature.

- Once the potatoes have finished cooking, drain, let cool, and dice. In a large bowl, combine the oil mixture, yogurt, lemon juice, green onions, and chives, and mix well. Season with salt and pepper to taste and gently stir in the potatoes.

- Refrigerate until ready to serve.

# Sage
# in the Kitchen

Sage leaves are extremely aromatic and should be used in moderation. However, the right amount adds a lot of flavor to meats, especially rabbit, poultry, pork and game. It a highly prized herb in Italian cuisine, where its used to flavor olives, minestrone soup, risotto, and one of Italy's most celebrated dishes, *osso buco*.

## Buying and Storing

When it is in season, fresh sage can be bought at the market, and most grocery stores carry it year-round, although it will not be locally-grown. The herb will keep for several days in the refrigerator with its stems in a glass of water or loosely wrapped in a damp paper towel. When buying dried sage, choose whole leaves over ground, and gently crush them before serving to keep their flavor.

If you have sage in your garden, select and pick a bunch with non-flowering branches and suspend it in a dry, dark, well-ventilated area for two or three weeks. To protect it from dust, cover it with a paper (not plastic) bag pierced with holes.

When the leaves start to fall off, rub the sage bouquet between your hands over a piece of parchment paper. Store in a glass jar with a lid. For infusions, keep the dried plants whole in a closed paper bag.

. . . . . . . . . . . . . . . . . . . . . . . . . . . . . . .

## Caution

La sauge contient une quantité non
Sage is rich in vitamin K, which is produced by the body as well as certain foods and necessary for the formation of blood clots. People taking anticoagulant medication should only eat small amounts of sage.

## Sage Pesto

Sage adds a unique twist to a classic Italian recipe!

### Ingredients

½ cup (125 ml) sage leaves

½ cup (125 ml) Parmesan cheese, grated

2 cloves garlic, minced

Zest and juice of 1 lemon

¼ cup (60 ml) olive oil

Salt and pepper to taste

### Preparation

- In a food processor, combine all the ingredients except the oil. Add oil in a slow, steady stream while pulsing.

- Serve with grilled slices of bread (crostinis) or over pasta.

# Sage-Roasted Chicken

Spreading herbed oil or butter under the skin flavors roast chicken and keeps it exquisitely moist and tender. In this recipe, the sage is so aromatic that no salt needs to be added.

## Ingredients for 4 or more

1 whole 3 lb chicken, legs tied and ready to cook

1 clove garlic, minced

12 fresh sage leaves, chopped

2 tbsp olive oil

Pepper

3 tbsp white wine

½ cup chicken stock

## Preparation

- Preheat the oven to 350°F (180°C).
- In a bowl, combine the garlic, sage, and oil. Mix well and season with pepper.
- Spread this mixture under the chicken skin and inside the cavity.
- Spread this mixture under the chicken skin and inside the cavity.
- Place the chicken in a roasting pan, put it in the oven and cook for 30 minutes.
- Pour 2 tbsp of the white wine over the chicken, cover with a sheet of parchment paper and cook for another 30 minutes.
- Remove the paper, add the rest of the wine, and cook for 30 minutes.
- To make the sauce, take the chicken out of the roasting pan and keep warm. Drain the cooking juices and keep them to make homemade stock. Deglaze the dripping pan with the chicken stock and reduce for a few minutes.
- Serve with steamed vegetables or a puree of root vegetables.

# Sage
# in the Kitchen

## Sage Saltimbocca

Another simple yet absolutely divine Italian dish made with sage.

### Ingredients for 4

4 thin veal cutlets

16 fresh sage leaves

4 slices prosciutto

2 tsp unsalted butter or non-hydrogenated margarine

2 tbsp olive oil

1 dried shallot, minced

½ cup (125 ml) white wine

½ cup (125 ml) 15% cooking cream

### Preparation

- Tenderize the cutlets with a meat tenderizer and cut each one in half to make 8 strips.
- Place two sage leaves on each strip and cover with ½ slice of prosciutto.
- Roll each strip into a tight spiral, using toothpicks to hold the rolls together.
- Heat a skillet, add the butter and oil, and cook the veal rolls over high heat for 2 to 4 minutes.
- Remove from the pan and keep warm.
- Soften the shallot in the cooking juices. Deglaze with white wine and reduce by half.
- Strain the sauce, return it to the pan, add the cream, and let it thicken.
- Remove the toothpicks and place two rolls on each plate. Spoon a bit of cream sauce over each serving.
- Delicious with roasted potatoes and braised endives.

# Thyme
## in the Kitchen

Thyme enhances sauces, stuffings, salads and fish. It also tastes lovely with vegetables as well as braised, roasted or grilled meats. A truly universal herb!

### Buying and Storing

Thyme sprigs, bouquets and bunches all keep very well for several weeks. After that, the leaves will start falling off. For long-term storage, let the leaves dry out in a container that "breathes," like a wicker basket, or hang upside-down in bouquets. When they have fully dried, rub the branches between your hands over wax paper to remove the leaves, remove all stem pieces that may have fallen, and store in a sealed container.

### Caution

People who are allergic to plants the La-miaceae family (mint family) should avoid thyme, and people who are sensitive to birch pollen or celery may also be sensitive to thyme. Some sources discourage pregnant or breastfeeding women from using thyme extracts and concentrates.

## Guinea Hen with Cider Thyme Glaze

Guinea hen in a light sauce is a delicious alternative to chicken. Use other herbs depending on what is in season—this dish is just as delicious with rosemary, sage, savory or tarragon.

### Ingredients for 4

1 Guinea hen, cut into pieces

Salt and pepper

1 large bunch thyme

2 garlic cloves, minced

5 tbsp olive oil

3 tbsp flour

3 tbsp butter

¾ cup (180 ml) cider

A few branches thyme to decorate

### Preparation

- Season the Guinea hen with salt and pepper and place the pieces in a large dish, making sure the pieces are not over apping.
- Marinate for 1 hour at room temperature or up to 4 hours in the refrigerator.
- Drain and dry the Guinea hen pieces. Strain the seasoned oil and set aside.
- Coat the pieces in flour. In a saucepan, heat the butter until foamy and brown the meat.
- Add the cider and the reserved olive oil.
- Cover and let simmer for 1 hour.
- Decorate with a few branches of thyme before serving.

# Table of Contents

Spiced Lamb ................................................................................ 150

Aioli ........................................................................................... 106

Asparagus with Chervil Cream ................................................. 128

Turmeric Avocado Spread ......................................................... 140

Quail with Juniper Berries ........................................................ 152

Pork and Potato Curry .............................................................. 144

Colombo Lamb .......................................................................... 122

Spiced Fruit Compote ............................................................... 116

Aromatic Apple Compote ......................................................... 132

Mango Star Anise Cream .......................................................... 112

Shrimp and Chive Sauté ........................................................... 130

Tandoori Fish ............................................................................. 141

Ginger Orange Salmon .............................................................. 154

Pepper-Crusted Filet Mignon ................................................... 180

Black Cumin Quinoa Cakes ...................................................... 138

Spiced Veal Burgers .................................................................. 176

Aniseed Nut Cake ...................................................................... 110

Chocolate Cinnamon Spice Cake ............................................. 118

Hungarian Goulash .................................................................... 168

Cauliflower Gratin ..................................................................... 164

Harissa ....................................................................................... 172

Creamy Hummus ....................................................................... 136

Rabbit with Two-Mustard Sauce .............................................. 162

**Spice Mixes** ........................................................................... 101

    Baharat ............................................................................. 101

    Berber ............................................................................... 101

    Cajun Seasoning .............................................................. 104

    Classic Curry .................................................................... 102

    Singapore Curry ............................................................... 103

    Chat Masala ...................................................................... 102

    Chinese Five-Spice ........................................................... 103

    Thai Red Curry Paste ....................................................... 105

Antillean Colombo ..................................................................... 104

# Table of Contents

Mussels in Green Peppercorn Sauce ................................................................ 179

Licorice Muffins ........................................................................................... 182

Baked Eggs with Celery Seeds ..................................................................... 126

Sage Pesto .................................................................................................. 190

Basil Pesto .................................................................................................. 114

Shrimp, Scallop and Ginger Pasta ................................................................ 156

Saffron Coconut Scallops ............................................................................ 186

Guinea Hen with Cider Thyme Glaze ........................................................... 194

Tomato Oregano Pizza ................................................................................. 166

Duck with Spicy Beer Sauce ........................................................................ 173

Greek Chicken ............................................................................................. 184

Carrot Coriander Soup ................................................................................. 134

Superfood soup ........................................................................................... 147

Green Vegetable and Tarragon Soup ........................................................... 148

Forty Clove Roast Chicken ........................................................................... 107

Indian Chicken with Pistachios .................................................................... 120

Sage-Roasted Chicken ................................................................................ 191

Warm Quinoa with Cranberries and Cashews ............................................. 117

Ratatouille Provençale ................................................................................. 158

Rice with Ginger and Peppers ..................................................................... 157

Light and Fresh Potato Salad ....................................................................... 188

Sage Saltimbocca ....................................................................................... 192

Sambal Olek ................................................................................................ 105

Salmon Gravlax with Dill ............................................................................. 108

Superfood Smoothie .................................................................................... 146

Lentil Soup .................................................................................................. 142

Two-Pepper Vegetable Soup ........................................................................ 178

Fish Pasta Medley ....................................................................................... 174

Tabbouleh ................................................................................................... 170

Carrot and Caraway Spread ......................................................................... 124

Spiced Tea .................................................................................................. 132

Tzatziki ....................................................................................................... 160

Tarragon Vinegar ........................................................................................ 148

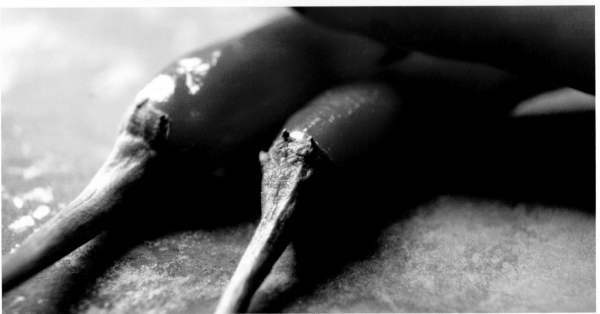